Is That It ?

Joan Toase

Amazon KDP

Acknowledgements

Revised second edition (US Trade)

Copyright © 2023 Joan Toase

All rights reserved

Edited by Mark Mcvittie

Cover photo copyright Shelagh Roberts

Interior photos copyright Joan Toase

Available in paperback from Amazon

ISBN: 9798848992601

Dedication

I dedicate this book to my family and friends, who unwittingly over the years, planted the seeds of these wee stories, which I hope you will enjoy and make you smile !

Order of Stories

Tales of Yesteryear:

Cold Comfort	10
Long, Long Time Ago	15
Blue Belle	22
String of Pearls	28
Mrs. Dunne	44
Miss Jean Baxter	46
Saturday Night Fever	50
Killowen Village on Carlingford Lough	53
Mrs. McNeice's School	65
Wait Te You Hear This One !	69
Portadown, Here We Come !	74

Family Years:

The Fortune Teller: The Big Night Out	80
The Fortune Teller: The Housekeeper	87
The Fortune Teller: Howareyizalldoin	92
No Kidding	96
Purple Herby's First Family	99
Purple Herby: A Mind of its Own	104
Purple Herby: On the Road Again	111
Fisherman's Friend	117
Hello Sailor !	119
A Load of Bull	127
The Chair	130

Retirement Years:

Come Day, Go Day	134
Vacation vs. Holiday	136
Hide and Souk	142
Icelandic Ash and After	147
Cash Only	161
Not Her Again !	166
Mind the No Parking Sign	169
Wee John	171
Pup's Song	173
Cat's Cradle	176
Isolation, Insomnia and I (Me !)	180
Our Charlie's Story	188
Big Boy Now	198

Further Reading:

Eddie Joe	200
Mrs. Morgan's Biscuits	204
Them and Us	207
The Flowers in May	214
Mr. McBride's Big Moment	216
D'Ye Mind the Day ?	220
Some Old Cures from Mourne !	222
When You Think About It !	224
Bible Cake Recipe	226

Tales of Yesteryear

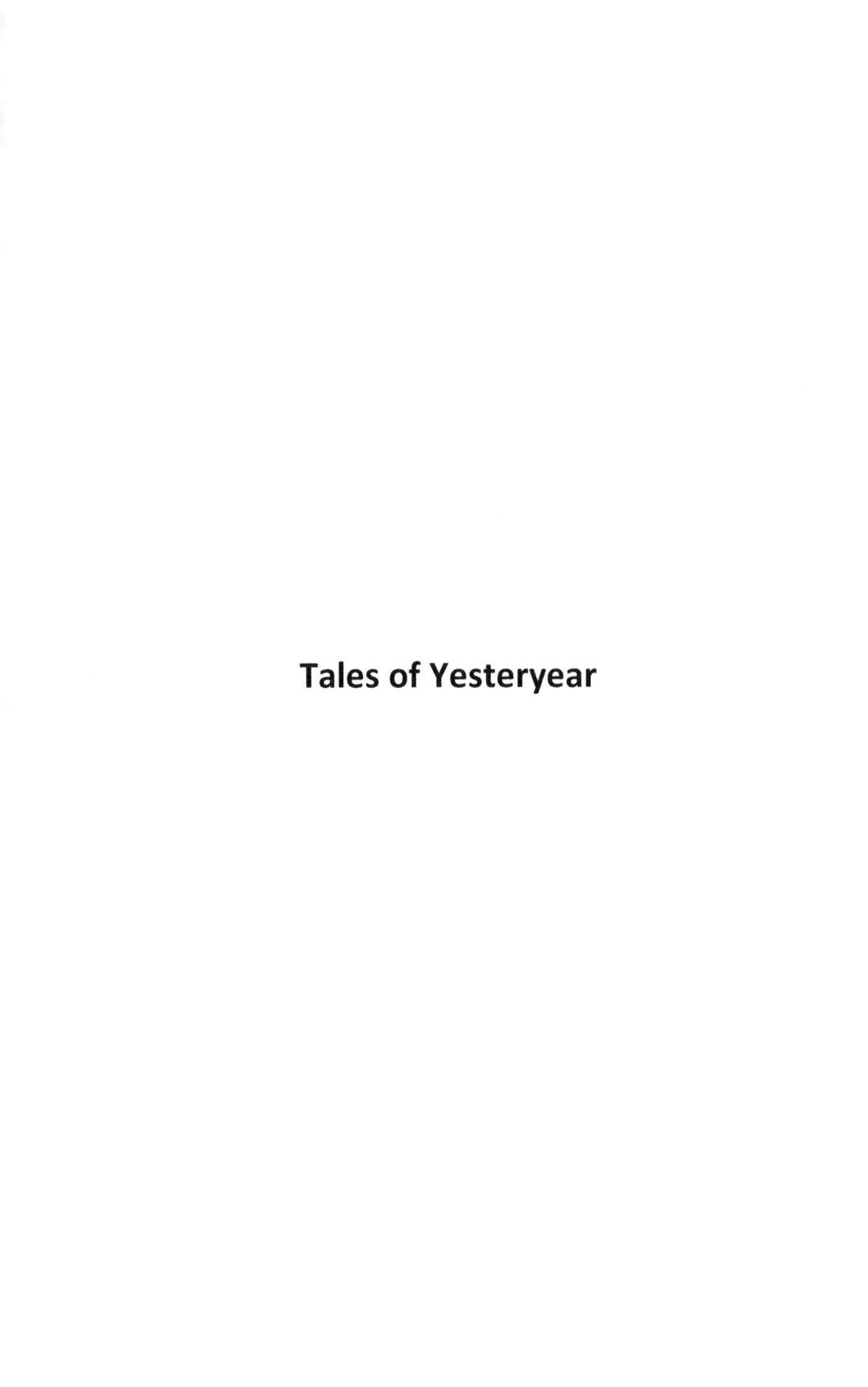

Cold Comfort

Well, there I was, up to my neck in expensive bubbles, topping up the hot water now and then with my big toe and thinking about nothing at all. ----------- Bliss !!

After a while, my thoughts strayed to the meeting I had been at the night before in the Lecture Hall in Rostrevor. Nice wee baldy man with glasses and a good clear voice had been telling us about climate change and how the Mournes all around us had been formed millions of years ago. He was dead sure of it and really passionate about his subject. Facinating stuff, how the melting ice had licked out long valleys and shifted mountain tops into place. Millions and trillions of years seemed to be just a couple of months to him, but sure maths or time were never my strong point and he had me really confused. He had the figures and slides to prove his theory.

Now, see me ? I had always thought God was responsible for the Silent Valley, Binnian, Slieve Martin, the Fairy Glen and all that. Anyway, when I thought about the Bloody Bridge that led on to thoughts about Maggie and the giant lep she took. That led on to the Dinnywater and the Cassywater and how they tumble down from the mountain, over the stones, through fertile fields and out into Carlingford Lough. Sure every drop of pure water has to come from somewhere ! Well then, there must have been wee men and women roaming the land, foundered in the ice and cold, looking for something to eat, millions of years ago, dear love them ! No matter what that man said, I still think God had something to do with it !!

Then I thought to myself, "Would you wise up, sure you know nothing about that lot ! Haven't you plenty of good family of your own who lived, farmed and died here in the Mournes ? Every last one of them had a story to tell of the times they lived in and it wasn't a million years ago."

Now here's my problem. Who will I write about ? All the old aunts, uncles, grannies, grandads and great grannies are all gone now. All under the Mourne soil. There's nobody left to ask. My own mother would have said "Ask Norah, she took an interest in family history." I should have asked Aunt Norah but sure I never thought of it. She could have told me of family wars over wee bits of land and farms, rows over right of ways, good marriages and wealth, poverty and emigration, bad marriages and lucky escapes.

She could have told me about the emigration to Australia of her aunt and uncle and their five children, times were bad and money was tight. He was a good enough small farmer and father but he got too fond of the drink. One monthly fair day he went into Kilkeel and met a man in a pub who told him Australia was a great place to make a quick fortune. After a few drinks he went to the agent and put the house and farm up for sale immediately, then he went home and told the wife that they were all leaving for a new life in Australia in a week. Wasn't that a lovely surprise for her ?

Anyway, she wasn't a Mourne woman for nothing ---- she could cope, five children and all, they sailed on the ferry from Greencastle to Greenore, then by the steam packet boat to Liverpool and joined the sailing ship for the six long weeks journey to their unknown life in Australia. As far as I know there are still strands of them farming there.

Great Aunt Eileen wouldn't have been much good on real family history. I think she would have only told me the nice genteel bits about those ancestors who had done well for themselves, like the uncle who had left Mourne at an early age and had become mayor of a remote northern Canadian town, och, maybe life in the fur trading and Indian settlements wasn't all fancy dinners and happiness. The mayor's chain might have been a bit of a langle (a langle is a bit of rope tied to an animal's leg to stop it straying, you know !) I hope his experience of life in Mourne stood him in good stead.

No, no, it's the nitty gritty bits I would like to have known about, especially the one about the good-looking youngest daughter of the big farmer in Ballintur. Apparently she would drive by pony and trap to Warrenpoint in time to take the new-fangled train to go shopping in Dublin ----- by heavens, that was something ! But then guess what ? She fell in love with one of the labouring sons of a poor family who lived away up the country. That caused a bit of a ruction I'm sure, for not only was he penniless but he was of the other sort too !! Not an easy one for any of them. Sure how could he keep a high maintenance one like that in the style she was accustomed and what would she know about keeping a family on a pittance ? No benefits or allowances in those days. Her old fellow didn't like it one bit and shipped her out to relations in ------ you guessed it ---- Australia. There she stayed for fifteen long years but her heart always stayed true to her Kilfeaghan man and Mourne. You know, I think he must have been very handsome, had good manners and could make her laugh, otherwise a girl like that wouldn't have taken him under her notice !

There's another piece of that story I'd like love to know about. What did she do all those years in Australia ? Did she just look pale and interesting sitting under a eucalyptus tree all day, dreaming of her lover and old Ireland or did she learn to shear sheep and get on with things ? See, there's so much that I don't know and how can I write a story not knowing the in-between bits.

Eventually, Belle came home to the farm in Ballintur and lived with her batchelor brother who had inherited the farm after the parents had died, only to discover that the love of her life was happily married to a wee girl from Attical and had seven children. Poor Belle became a recluse and never put her foot outside the farm gate again. You know, if a fellow couldn't wait fifteen or twenty years for you, then maybe you'd be better off without him ! Belle lies in Knotty Ash Graveyard in Rostrevor with the rest of her family.

What about the boyo who owned the scutch mill ? He up and married a young one just months after the wife died.

She was pretty and much younger than some of his sons and daughters. They gave her a hard time in case she produced offspring and they lost their inheritance. Oh, there's a big story there, I'm sure it was the talk of the country !

Then there was the story of the lad who set fire to the byres and outhouses because he couldn't stand the sight of another bloody cow calving in the middle of the night ! He ran away to sea and was never heard of for years until one day an elegant, dark-skinned lady arrived in Kilkeel by limousine to trace her ancestors. Oh, how I wish I knew of his adventures ! Did he ever think of the Silent Valley or the Deer's Meadow ? Did he remember the fishing boats at the harbour ?

That wee man has a lot to answer for with his millions and trillions of years. I realised the bubbles were up to the top of the bath and the water was running cold so there was nothing for it only to pull out the plug. The water started gushing down the drain along with my thoughts and dreams of other people's lives. As I watched, lots of tiny bubbles stuck to the side of the bath. Maybe this is like the people who lived in Mourne a long time ago, in that they left their mark and memories behind.

Long, Long Time Ago

A long, long time ago in the hills away above Rostrevor village in County Down there lived a sheep farmer. He was a shy lonely man who had looked after his elderly parents until they died. He did have brothers and sisters but they had all married and moved away. He was a good son but as he grew older he was sad living on his own, with only his trusted sheepdog Lucky to keep him company.

In the clear evenings when he had finished working with his animals and he was in his garden doing a bit of tidying up, he could see the smoke rising and lights coming on in the houses in the village, way below in the valley. He thought how nice it would be if he had a family and somebody to talk to. He often thought he could hear children laughing and singing around his farmhouse but when he went outside to look there was nobody there. One day when he was down in the village buying his provisions, he heard somebody sing a strange song. The melody was catchy but the words bothered him and he kept thinking about them on his long walk home. "Will you still love me, will you still need me, when I'm sixty-four ?"

Now all this happened at least a hundred years before the Beatles made this song famous, so children, remember that music survives and lives a lot longer than we do !!

Well, when the farmer, whose name was John

Moffatt, began to think about the song he realised that now he was SIXTY-TWO years old and that he had NOBODY to love or be loved by ! That gave him only two years to find somebody ---- and Lucky, the old sheepdog had no family either, what should they do ?

Maybe after the ewe's had lambed in early Spring and things were quiet he thought he might take a dander down to the village and not rush back up the hill as he always did. Maybe he'd get talking to somebody other than the vet or Mrs. Johnston, who owned the grocery shop. He was a very shy man and he just couldn't bring himself to talk to strangers. He was comfortable with the farmers and locals that he knew all his life but he never stayed around long enough to chat much with anyone ! True, he went down to the village most Sunday mornings to church, said his prayers and slipped out before any of the congregation could stop to have a chat with him. People did try but it only seemed to embarrass him, so John just disappeared back up the mountain path as quickly as he could !

Spring came and went, the ewe's lambed as they always did, poor old John would rush down to buy his weekly provisions and forget all about finding somebody to love. Too late when he was back up at the house, he would remember that he should have stayed on for a while in the village. "Ahh well", he thought, "Sure I'll have to go back down soon again, I could do with a new pair of boots before the bad weather sets in."

A few weeks later he and Lucky headed down to the village to call at Mr. O'Hare's draper's shop. Of course, Mr. O'Hare knew John well (and his Mammy and Daddy before him !) He soon had John fixed up with good strong boots made with chrome leather and sparable soles, thick socks, a nice pair of hard-wearing tan corduroy trousers, with a matching check shirt and left them on the counter. He suggested that John should go down the street to Barney the barber's shop and get his hair cut, now that he was down in the village.

When John called back to collect his parcel, Mr. O'Hare (good salesman that he was !) asked John to try on the trousers and shirt again to make sure they were right for him and that the strong boots fitted well. When John looked in the shop mirror, he couldn't believe that the handsome fellow looking back was himself !! He smiled and thought, "This is going to cost me an awful lot of money but sure I've never spent anything foolishly in my life and now that I'm sixty-two maybe it's time that I did !"

Lucky, who was tied up outside the shop door looked in and barked loudly. Poor Lucky looked so bedraggled and uncared for that Mr. O'Hare tactfully suggested that John take him across the road to the vet's assistant and get him groomed too, meanwhile he would ask his wife Mrs. O'Hare, who lived with him upstairs over the shop to make them all something nice to eat to celebrate the makeover !

When Mrs. O'Hare heard what was happening she

filled the big saucepan with lovely new potatoes, chopped some cabbage and onions fresh from the garden into another pan and made an apple pie. She knew that she had a nice big piece of boiled ham left from yesterday with some cheese sauce and thought it would do them all very nicely !!

    Mrs. O'Hare had often wondered about that man living away up there on his own. She remembered that at one time it was a busy farm with kind, hard-working parents, the children had grown up and emigrated because of lack of work here in the area. This young man John, she remembered had stayed on to help his elderly parents, because he was needed at home. Other isolated farm dwellings near John's had slipped into disrepair, as one by one the families had died off and the young people moved away. Emigration, for there was no work for young people, sure it was happening all over Ireland at that time. "Poor man" she thought, "He never had the chance to go places or meet anyone. What girl would want to go away up to that lonely place to live, no neighbours and only the sheep or crows to talk to !" Here was a chance to help him, if she could but first she had to make friends with him.

    Mrs. O'Hare called down to her husband in the shop below that the meal would be ready in about an hour. She knew that it would take more than a few minutes for him to finish up with his customer and coax John into joining them for a meal. John, meanwhile had decided that he liked the look of his "New me" and the new look of Lucky, who looked like a young agile dog again. He paid his bill quite happily and for once didn't argue over the price.

"Well", thought John, "Here's a whole new experience waiting for me, I'd better not waste it." He thanked Mr. O'Hare kindly and said he'd be delighted to stay. John had been well brought up and he knew it was good manners to bring a small gift. He thought he would walk down the street and see if he could find anything suitable. Maybe Mrs. O'Hare would like a nice box of chocolates. Next door to O'Hare's was the village post office, where you could buy nearly everything, minerals, cigarettes, sweets, stamps, notepaper, envelopes, cough mixture, carbolic soap, cocoa for making hot drinks, fresh eggs -------- oh, you name it and Jimmy, the postmaster could get it for you !

"Is that yourself, John ?" said Jimmy, trying not to look surprised when the smart, well-dressed man appeared at the counter. John tried to be chatty and talk about the weather and the price of everything but Jimmy knew fine well John was not here to discuss the weather ! Jimmy was complaining that business was bad, nearly as bad as the farming had been last year.

After some more general chat John confided that the O'Hare's had asked him to stay and have his tea with them and his difficulty was deciding what to bring to the O'Hare's as a wee gift. Jimmy thought this was unusual but he knew Mrs. O'Hare was a kindly soul, who had probably taken pity on poor John, knowing her husband had sold him a whole new wardrobe and made a new man of him. "Well now, let me think", said Jimmy. He looked at his shelves and remembered that Mrs. O'Hare had been in the other day looking for a new teapot but he hadn't any in stock. He suddenly remembered there might be one out in the back store that hadn't seen the light of day for years.

"Mind the shop for a minute will you, John" and with that Jimmy went out of the side door. In two minutes he was back with the cutest prettiest teapot that you'd ever seen ! He gave it a quick shine up with a duster and showed it to John, who thought it was just the very thing. Jimmy found a box that fitted the teapot, wrapped it up in brown paper and John paid for it without looking for a luck penny !!

"My goodness, all this new experience is going to my head", thought John, "But sure I feel great !" Back he went to O'Hare's shop just as Mr. O'Hare was closing up. "Come on in, John", said Mr. O'Hare, who was putting his books and cash into the safe. "The wife will be calling us upstairs in a minute and she will have something for Lucky too."

John presented Mrs. O'Hare with his gift and she was so overcome, that a wee tear rolled down her face. "Imagine that lonely man being so kind", she thought, "How did he know that I wanted a new teapot, he could not have brought me anything nicer !" "How did the O'Hare's know that being invited for a meal would mean so much to me", thought John.

After that every time John was down in the village he called in to visit the O'Hare's. Well, that was the start of a great friendship and you know it wasn't long before Mrs. O'Hare's young niece Alice began to drop in at the same time to see her aunt and that was the start of another close friendship with a happy ending !

    By the time John was sixty-four the Beatles song had an answer to the question and the quiet house up on the hill was ringing with love and laughter !

Blue Belle

I'm an old lady now, they tell me. Am I ? I don't know. I feel the same as I always did. The dark hair may be well streaked with grey now but these days hair streaked any colour is fashionable and doesn't label anyone. If I am old now, soon I will be VERY OLD and not able to remember any of Great Aunt Belle's story. Perhaps I should put together the patches of stories about her that have passed down through the generations of my family.

Belle was the youngest daughter of a prosperous farmer and his wife, they owned a sizeable acreage of land between the Mourne Mountains and Carlingford Lough. The family, mother, father and several small children had earlier left Ireland for a new life in Australia, where one child died. Records have it that they travelled on to New Zealand, stayed there a few years where Isabella, known as Belle, was born.

Having made money there, they returned home, bought a farm of land and Victorian farmhouse at Ballintur, between Rostrevor and Kilkeel, called Daisy Hill. Another daughter, Elizabeth was born there but died when aged only three. There were plenty of cousins nearby to visit, neighbours and farmworkers children to play with, animals in the yard to make friends with and endless adventures in the surrounding countryside. The mountains and seashore were only a stone's throw away. It was an idyllic place to grow up and grow up they did.

Two of the older brothers went off to Canada and a third went back to Australia for a while. There was great rejoicing when the eldest girl, Mabel, married a suitable young man from a neighbouring farm near Kilkeel. Little sister Belle was a constant visitor to their home, where there was always something exciting happening. Life now at home with the parents and studious older sister was boring. The lessons she received from her teacher went in one ear and out of the other, time-consuming she thought, when she could have been out running free as the wind.

When Mabel's babies started to arrive with startling frequency, Belle was ecstatic. Never would there be such a devoted aunt as she ! After the fourth baby arrived, in less than as many years, the young wife struggling to keep the home and children organised was perpetually tired, irritable and depressed. James, the young husband began to feel neglected, unwanted and took to the drink, not an unusual thing to happen !

Farming in Ulster was going through another bad spell at that time, prices were low, with small return for endless hard work. Cattle and sheep were hard to sell but still had to be fed and that cost money. One day he went into the town, Kilkeel, for the monthly fair and had little luck selling his stock. He met a man in the pub who told him that Australia was now the place to be. Fortunes could be made by anyone who had an ounce of farming sense, many Ulster farmers were there already, the man said. After a few drinks, James headed off to the local auctioneer's office and put the farm, house and stock up for auction immediately. It seemed a wonderful idea. Home he went, in great form and told his wife that they were leaving the next week for a new life in Australia ! Some of their relations had already moved there a few years earlier.

Well, that was a bombshell alright ! When the panic began to wear off, Mabel realised that perhaps it would help their marriage back to stability, for she loved him dearly. She would cope no matter how hard the work, although she didn't understand at the time the enormity of what they were taking on. After a hectic few days preparation and tearful farewells, they left Kilkeel with their children and their scant belongings, boarded the ferry from nearby Greencastle, which took them across the lough to Greenore. The mail boat left from there for Liverpool, where they joined the big ship for the long six-week journey to their unknown life Down Under. The same journey that Mabel had made as a child with her parents years before.

Belle was growing up too and becoming a beautiful if not wilful young lady, fond of her own way. Her mother and father despaired of her becoming a desirable bride, even with a sizable dowry, for any respectable young man of substance. Her mother tried to encourage her on shopping trips to Dublin but she had little interest in culture, music, style or anything that a young lady of her standing should have. Now that her siblings had left home, she roamed the countryside by herself, dressed in old clothes and strong boots. She visited tenant farmers and their families in their humble dwellings, not as a daughter of the wealthy but as their friend and was made welcome. Her father tried to dissuade her from these solitary rambles, for he was worried by who she would meet or be influenced by. There was much unrest in the land and the old sectarian troubles were brewing under the surface.

Belle developed a special friendship with one of the sons of a family whom she visited, several miles up the country. Not only was he penniless but he was of the other persuasion too. Recipe for disaster in those days ! He was a very kind sensible and handsome young man with a good sense of humour, no wonder Belle was head over heels in love with him. He had fallen in love with Belle too, although he realised that she was out of his reach and he could never provide for her, in the way that she had been reared. He knew that someday if he could get out of this country, he could work as hard as any man, make his fortune and come back to claim Belle for his own. How would her old man like that, he often wondered. Belle, on the other hand wanted Phil and what Belle wanted she usually got !

A year passed with the lovers meeting occasionally, secretly in remote parts of the area. Belle had tried to cajole her father into meeting Phil after her father heard rumours of the romance. During that time, a flock of sheep were stolen from their pasture on the mountain and rightly or wrongly, some of Phil's family were blamed. By now Belle's parents were worried about her involvement with these people, bringing disgrace on them all.

Only one thing to be done, her father thought. He quickly made arrangements for her to stay with her sister in Australia. Belle went happily, understanding that it was just for a short visit. She had missed her sister so much and was longing to see the children, who by now had two new little brothers. She was sure that somehow her romance with Phil would resolve itself while she was away. She hoped that he might even come to Australia to find her but she had completely overlooked the fact that he didn't have money to travel to Newry, never mind halfway around the world !

Belle duly arrived in Melbourne and joined her family who were adapting well to this pioneering style of life. There she settled in, enjoying life, helping with the children on the farm and enjoying the company of her sister, while waiting on money for her passage home which her father had promised to send.

She was there for Mabel when James died from tetanus, he had kept his promises before leaving home that he would work hard and provide a good life for them. Later, when ten-year-old Luke was drowned while trying to save his pony from flash floods, Belle was there to comfort them. Eventually, the money arrived and it was time for Belle to return home. Home to the big house in Ballintur, home to nurse the elderly parents until they died, home to look after the unmarried brother who had inherited the farm.

Phil ? He had married a girl from the next parish and had six children. Of course, they lived in poverty but his wife knew how to manage on the little they had. When Belle heard the news she was devastated, saying if a fellow couldn't wait fifteen or twenty years, then he wasn't worth having !

Poor Belle became a recluse, never leaving the house or yard, speaking only to the animals, seldom to her brother and always disappeared should neighbours or relations chance to visit. Although she was harmless, the local children were afraid of her. They used to spy on her from the laneway and fields near the house, call her names and run away. Perhaps that's when people first called her "Blue Belle", maybe because of the pretty wild flowers that grew in the laneway or because of her depression.

When her brother was killed in a road traffic accident near their home, poor distraught Belle was admitted to Downpatrick mental asylum and the farm was sold. On winter nights, they say Belle's ghost still walks the lonely roads around Kilfeaghan and Ballymaderphy, keening for her lost love. She is buried in Knotty Ash graveyard, Rostrevor, beside her parents, brother and the little sister who died in childhood.

Well that's Belle's story ! I may have forgotten bits though and if I can remember then maybe it's not too late to stitch together another bit of my Moffatt family patchwork of stories. ("Cold Comfort" has more about Belle)

String of Pearls

Remember Glen Miller ? He was the American service man who had the big band, played fabulous music, nostalgic memories for hundred and thousands of young service people and their partners during the second world war and long after it. Music that still brings a smile or a tear to the eye of many. All those who danced to the real Major Glen Miller big band, jived to "Chattanooga Choo-choo" and "American Patrol", jitterbugged to "In the Mood" or smooched to "Moonlight Serenade", "Blueberry Hill" or "String of Pearls" will remember it all. Our song.

Well, let me tell you a true story, and it mostly is, although a few names have been changed ! It's about a wee girl from Killowen.

It was wartime, around 1943 and the American army was based at Ballyedmond estate. They had a big camp there, full of these handsome young soldiers in smart uniform. Some were city slickers but most were from rural farming and country areas, first time away from home, lonely, missing family, girlfriends and mom's apple pie. They were stuck in a strict unfamiliar routine in a foreign country and not quite able to understand the lingo even though it was English. Try translating to American English "Aye, he's a right lukin' fella sure enough", they hadn't a clue what we were talking about. True, they were right looking fellas ------- well, most of them anyway !

This girl was called Brigid, she had it all, outgoing sunny personality, tall, good figure, wonderful auburn hair and beautiful skin. Killowen girls all have good skin, I think it has something to do with all the wet weather we have ! Brigid had a good education and easily found a responsible job in the red cross department when she completed her training there. There were many civilians employed in the camp and it was a great boon to the local economy. Many of the girls found romance and quite a few found husbands there too ! Brigid loved her work and being part of all the activity that Ballyedmond camp and the surrounding area brought to the war effort. It was as if wee quiet Killowen had become another state of America, even some of the locals had acquired a Yankee drawl and they had never been further than Warrenpoint or Newry !!!

Naturally Brigid attracted attention from the soldiers but she was not easily impressed having been brought up by a strict but loving father, Danny, (her mother had died when she was born) two sisters, five brothers, numerous aunts, uncles and cousins. She knew when the boys were having her on, pulling her leg, taking the micky or whatever, she could give as good as she got and win ! Work was hard and shifts were long but there were many compensations ! One guy was constantly around in the background, he seemed quiet and good mannered, not as loud and noisy as his friends. He didn't contribute to the banter but seemed to enjoy her light-hearted answers. Brigid's family weren't all that happy with her working at the camp, after all she was the baby of the family and dear only knows who she could meet among all those strangers. At least she was able to come home every evening because they lived only a mile or so from the camp and the money was good - very good, compared with what she would have made locally.

She was a great help about the home and anything else her father needed a hand with. Still, she was getting bossy and a bit "yankeefied", as they would say round here. The big sisters were both courting local fellows and seemed happy enough but they couldn't help being curious about Brigid's work with the red cross at the camp and the glamour of being involved in the war effort with all these handsome men. Brigid always seemed to have something exciting happen at work and kept the family enthralled every evening with her stories when she came home.

Her father, though, was getting a bit fed up with her colourful accounts, the name-dropping of sergeant this and lieutenant that and her new way of speaking. "If I hear 'Aww gee Pop, that's mighty fine' or ----- 'You guys like some more tea ?' One more time, there's no telling what I'll ------ !" he often said, before he made his way out to the yard to escape another long story about how wonderful these Americans were.

The American forces were generous, of that there was no doubt. Brigid legally brought home lots of goodies. She happily brought cigarettes for all the smokers at home, spearmint chewing gum, new-fangled coffee in tins, candy for the wee cousins, canned orange juice by the gallon. Now and then the girls were given nylon stockings, all the way from America, such unheard of luxury ! While everyone enjoyed the benefits of Brigid's labour there was this feeling in the family that she was leaving them way behind, having more in common with her new friends and way of life.

Eventually the quiet guy became her special friend. He had a dependable, open and trustworthy nature. That's why his buddies nicknamed him "Trusty Rusty" ! It wasn't long before Brigid realised he was falling in love with her but at this stage romance was not on her agenda, enjoying work and just having a good time socially was quite enough. She had known some of the girls who worked in the canteen all her life and soon had made friends with others in different departments.

Because she lived so near the camp she could live at home and cycle to work every day. That was fine at the start but soon she envied the girls who were billeted at the camp in their own army female quarters. A few of the girls had romances going on with the soldiers and some had even got engaged ! Life was exciting at Ballyedmond ! When he was off-duty Rusty used to wait out the Kilkeel road a bit, beyond sight of the guard house to escort Brigid on her way home, it became a regular occurrence a couple of evenings a week. Brigid was glad of the company because the country roads were very dark, no street lighting then. They chatted, exchanged ideas about things and got to know each other better.

Every time Brigid was late home for tea the family interrogated her but she always had the last word. Music was Rusty's big interest. He always knew the latest pop song, the names of all the bands and singers, even the writers. He had a good voice and could play the guitar a bit too. Glen Miller was his favourite by miles. Neighbours began to notice Miss Brigid Mulligan dawdling home on the road with a Yank pushing her bike. People talk !!

"You better bring that fella home for tea, if he's that great, before Da catches you down the loanin," her big sister told her with a smirk. Brigid didn't take any notice for she knew her Da would give him a rough time and the boys would only take a hand out of him. She didn't like the thought of him and his accent being made fun of.

Big sister kept at it and a few weeks later she asked Rusty if he would like to come home with her and have a meal. They decided Wednesday would be fine. Brigid knew that the monthly fair day in Kilkeel was on and that her father had a few cattle to sell. There was a good chance that he would fall in with some of the other farmers and be home late enough for Rusty to meet the rest of the family and be halfway back to the camp !

Needless to say, Danny arrived in just as the spuds were placed on the table. After a bit of general chat, Danny showing great interest in Rusty's background began probing about the American's family. He let Rusty know in no uncertain terms about the long line of very devout, honest hardworking farmers he came from and this family of his were part of. "The family who pray together stay together", he told him solemnly. Danny could see out of the corner of his eye that Brigid was looking at Rusty, her face glowing with admiration and he knew with a sinking feeling that this was for real, remembering the love he had for his late wife.

"We don't want to lose her to Illinois ---- where ever the Hell that is, I'll have to put a stop to this", he thought. "How often do you go to chapel, Rusty ?" he asked with a smile, "Why, I don't rightly know, Sir" replied the young man. "Ain't never been, see us folks don't go for that mumbo jumbo stuff. Paw says, 'Keep out of that, Junior, paddle your own canoe, do the best you can for other folks and keep your hands clean.' No Siree Bob, God don't figure a lot with my kin ! We live a long way off the track and I guess we get along mighty fine without him -----".

Well, that was a conversation stopper if ever there was one in the Mulligan household. Poor Brigid, she wanted to die then and there but first she had to get Rusty out safely before he was booted out. She left him up the loanin a bit, without his goodnight kiss, remembering the way her father had pushed his chair back from the table and stomped out to the yard, without saying anything to anybody. Brigid crept back into the kitchen with a heavy heart and helped her sister finish drying the dishes, neither spoke.

Out in the byre Danny smiled grimly to himself. "I knew it, I knew it !" he thought. "Too bloody good to be wholesome. A Baptist or a Presbyterian American would have been bad enough -------- I would've had to houl it and never let on to the country ----- but a bloody atheist ? Thank God I found out in time."

Rusty was quite unaware he had put his "fut" in it, as they say here, up to his oxter. He knew that Brigid was on her day off next day and he was going with his platoon on manoeuvres in the mountains, for a tiring couple of hard days and nights training.

Brigid spent a lot of time thinking about Rusty. She was a clever girl with a logical outlook on life. She made a list of all the things she loved about Rusty, below that a list of all the things she didn't, below that a list of all the things she wasn't too sure about. On another page she made a list of things she was definite about and below that a whole lot of things that confused her. Then she put her pencil through the lot. Brigid prayed as she never prayed before but still her situation didn't get any clearer.

It was at least a week before Rusty set eyes on her, even though he had made many excuses to pass the Nissan hut where her office was. He immersed himself in his music in off duty times. One tune seemed to follow him around and meet him at every corner. It was called "String of Pearls", a simple haunting melody.

Meal times at the Mulligan farmhouse had lost their sparkle. Brigid's stories were scant, few and far between when she was there. She seemed to work late a lot and everyone knew the war had taken a sinister turn. It was all bad news, doom and gloom from the war front. Things lightened up a bit when it was rumoured that General Patton "Old Blood and Guts" was coming to rally the troops. Lots of extra training, work, spit and polish were demanded to make the troops and Ballyedmond camp "The best God damned American outfit in the country !"

He arrived suddenly one day in Ballyedmond at the camp in this most beautiful area. After inspecting the troops, knowing that soon these boys would be in great danger and many lives would be lost, to boost their moral he announced that a grand ball had been arranged at the prestigious Great Northern Hotel in Rostrevor. The camp was agog with excitement, especially among the female staff. Who was going to get a formal invitation or would it only be for the higher ranks ? Could anyone go ? If one was lucky enough to be invited by a partner what on earth would one wear ? Ball gowns weren't high on the list of necessities in wartime.

Rusty couldn't wait to present Brigid with an invitation. She was secretly hoping he would ask her first although she was sure one or two of the other G.I.'s that she knew would offer to take her. It was to be a really grand affair, with all the uncertainty and impending doom of war it just what was needed to give civilians and troops a much-needed lift.

Brigid's main worry after she received Rusty's invitation, like any girl, any time was what to wear. Nothing in her wardrobe, her sisters or her aunts that she could borrow would be suitable and she was determined to be the "belle of the ball" !! She knew that the local dressmakers would all be swamped with orders from her friends for dresses to be made or remade. "Make do and mend" was the slogan used everywhere as clothes were rationed and required coupons to buy. The allocation of coupons was very strict and used only for essential clothing so frivolous ball gowns were out of the question for most people. Brigid had an idea. She went to visit an old friend of her mother's. This lady had been a wonderful seamstress years ago for the gentry, in the days when there were many formal balls and beautiful fabrics to choose from for gowns. Mary was delighted to see Brigid and thrilled to be asked to help.

"I might be a bit slow now but I know how to make these things properly and it will be good to see if I can still do it ! Sure when this war's over the wimmen will be going mad for new dresses, it will be a bit of practice for me !" she said, "Now, what kind of material have you got and when do you want it made for ?" Brigid had to admit that she had no fabric yet but her Aunt Margaret said she might have a bit upstairs that would do, "Margaret, Margaret, that auld beesom, sure she wouldn't have anything next or near the kind of thing I'm used to working with." Her voice got higher and higher with excitement and Brigid realised that she had forgotten about an old feud between her aunt and Mary.

Brigid explained how much she was looking forward to this event, the first ball she had ever been asked to and how much it meant to be Rusty's partner at it. Mary listened to the young girl and realised that this dress could be the passport to a new life for Brigid. The old woman sized her up and down, turned her sideways, stretched her arms out wide, made her stand up on a wee stool, sit down and cross her ankles. Not a word was spoken, then she disappeared out of the room for at least five long minutes. Mary returned in triumph holding a big roll of pure silk, the colour of the winter sky on a sunny day. Brigid gasped and jumped up. "Mary, Mary, you can't cut that up for me, I won't let you!"

The old woman laughed and holding up the roll of fabric in her arms waltzed around the room "Brigid Mulligan, I can and I will! It's mine and I'll do whatever I like with it and it's a damn sight better than anything yer auld Aunt Margaret ever had or ever will!! Anyway, I owe it to your mother for she made me buy it years ago in Fosters in Newry. I was going to a big dance with a fella from Attical but we fell out before I got the dress made. It was a lucky escape for me, for he was no good but I kept the lovely material. Now I can repay your mother who was my best friend. Go on home now and come back next week."

Brigid kept a low profile at home, she gave them no information. Sunday came and they all went to Mass as usual, Danny leading the way, straight as a ramrod and the family trailing behind him like Brown's cows. On the way out in the crowd Brigid overheard one of the girls from work asking her sister what colour of a dress was Brigid going to wear to the ball. "First I heard of it" her sister replied, "She never said anything to me about it ! Anyway, she would need a special dress. I think the romance is all off, for there is no talk of him at all now." The other girl looked at her in disbelief and the penny dropped. "Big Sister is jealous" Maureen thought, "Thon fellow of hers doesn't work at the camp so they wouldn't get an invitation anyway. I saw Brigid talking to Rusty today behind the canteen and it didn't look all over to me," Maureen quietly answered.

The girls who stayed in female quarters invited Brigid to come to their dormitory to get ready for the ball and stay the night with them afterwards. They knew it would be difficult for her to rush home, get fed, washed, makeup and hair done and get back to the camp (on the bike !) In time to catch the transport laid on to take them all to the Great Northern Hotel. Brigid hadn't told anyone of the difficulties at home over Rusty. Everyone at work thought he was so kind and just plain nice, it broke her heart that he was not really accepted by her family. She was delighted to join the girls for that made the preparations so much more fun. Mary had surpassed herself and made Brigid the most perfect dress in two days with only one fitting ! She certainly hadn't lost her touch even with the arthritic fingers.

It was absolute chaos in the small dormitory with twelve excited girls all preparing, lending, borrowing and advising each other over every detail, trying to pool the best of what they had and time was moving on. Brigid had arrived with her small overnight bag, in which she had carefully packed her dress and covered it with paper. She told the family at the last minute that she had to attend a big conference concerning work and would stay overnight. No need to let on about music and nice dresses !!

Brigid waited until the girls had put on their finery and were all busy with the very last minute make up and adjustments. She had spent ages brushing her dark auburn hair into a pageboy style and then slipped into the wonderful shimmery, swirly silk dress.

There was a scream from Helen, "Oh, my God ! Look at Brigid. She's fabulous ! Look, look !" Everyone turned around and there she was ---- like a "million dollar babe" ! Belle of the ball before it began !

Coats on against the chilly night air, the girls filed out to the waiting transport. There was a rush as boy claimed girl, some of the more sophisticated types had managed to procure a corsage of flowers for their date in the traditional American way. Brigid found Rusty, who produced a corsage of cream camellias (bribed from the Ballyedmond gardener at the castle !) Which was perfect for the pale blue gown. After the welcoming speeches by the top brass, General Patton got into his stride and everyone knew they were in for a tough time ahead, heads were held higher, hands were held tighter, "A high price would have to be paid but America would save the world and future generations would live in golden peace. Yes, sir ---- God bless America !"

The music started, a sea of colour mixed with khaki swayed and filled the large ballroom. Rusty was the proudest guy there, holding Brigid in his arms dancing together, he knew she was the only girl for him and that the other guys knew he was one lucky son of a gun ! She was some looker, no dumb blonde was his Brigid ! He loved the colour of her hair and that dress was so beautiful but he felt that there was something missing, something, something -------- suddenly he knew what it was. That sweetheart neckline needed some jewellery, not just the pale camellias.

"They are playing our tune again, 'String of Pearls'. Honey" he whispered to her, "Will you marry me ?" They slithered to a stop on the well-polished floor, she looked at him with a grin, "Thought you'd never ask ! I can't say yes just now but ask me again in six months."

The first opportunity Rusty had after the dance he bought Brigid an expensive double string of pearls. They were the genuine ones with a solid silver clasp studded with tiny diamonds but her happiness was clouded because she couldn't show them off at home. Rusty was posted to France two days after he gave her the pearls. She tried to be lighthearted about it, the folks at home knew she had changed, something was wrong but she wouldn't say what was troubling her. She couldn't settle to anything and was sharp with people. She needed a change, somewhere where Rusty could come to if he got a sudden twenty-four hour leave and they could be together. Killowen was too far away from anywhere. Danny watched her every move and knew she was worried about something, "Maybe he had been too hard on her over the Yankee fella" he thought.

One morning at work her superior called her into his office. "Miss Mulligan, you are a young lady with great potential and I am happy to recommend you for a senior position," he said. "This position is not here at Ballyedmond but at the U.S. army training base, Langford Lodge beside Lough Neagh, near Crumlin and close to the air base. You'll do the same kind of work that you are trained for but in a senior capacity. Think about it and let me know." Like lightening she replied, "Sir, I have no need to think about it. When do I leave?"

Within a week Brigid had said goodbye to family, friends, relations and headed off to her new assignment. She settled in well, made new friends and wrote to Rusty every day. She bought some of Glen Miller's gramaphone records, lots of Artie Shaw's music and Vera Lynn's love songs because by now she had bought a small gramaphone as her own knowledge and love of music was increasing. She wore a smart black suit to her office every day and her pearls were the only jewellery she ever wore.

She was wearing the smart black suit one morning when the G.I. padre called her aside and told her that Rusty had been killed in action. Brigid was heartbroken, devastated, a total wreck. The American padre had taken her gently aside, told her about Rusty's death in France along with several of his comrades who had been stationed at Ballyedmond with him and what little he knew of the incident. Rusty's name was not on any of the communicants' list that he could source. "He promised that he would come back to Langford for me, we'd go to New York when this was all over and he would show me where all the film stars live. We'd have a house with a swimming pool ------- and now he's gone ----", she sobbed. The padre admired this beautiful Irish girl with her strong faith, pleasant manner and quick wit. He had met her many times in the course of his pastoral duties and always found her most helpful. He prepared men for difficult decisions, both spiritually and physically, when they needed help and reassurance. War casualties were not always fatal but often had unexpected outcomes.

Sadly, Brigid struggled on with her workload, which was growing by the day, eventually deciding that she needed to go back home. She thought the peace and quietness of a walk on Killowen beach would clear her head, which she so recently would have thought boring but was now the panacea that she craved. Brigid knew well that she was not the only one suffering loss of a boyfriend, husband, fiancé or even an illicit lover and was ashamed of her weakness. She had teasingly not given Rusty the answer he had expected to his proposal and she had not been given the second chance to say yes. "There y'are now", she thought, "That's what you get for being too smart and me only stalling for time, for I knew it would be a straight choice between him and our ones. All I have now are my memories, dreams of what might have been and my string of pearls."

Two weeks later Brigid had all the time she wanted to walk on Killowen beach and with a clear head decided that perhaps she was not ready for American life or America for her !! "Maybe there's something to be said for knowing the seed breed and generation of a prospective husband, as long as he wasn't a farmer ------- no way would she have a bucket over her arm or make tea for half the country at harvest time but on the other hand, if I loved him the way I loved Rusty --- Oh gee, who knows ? There's more to life and I've just to get on with it."

    And she did.

Mrs. Dunne

I'm a Rostrevor girl, born and bred. I remember some notable characters from around the village and beyond from away back ! Did you know that the vast shopping empire known as Dunne's Stores was founded by the entrepreneur Ben Dunne, whose mother owned a wee draper's shop here in Bridge Street ?

    Yes, Mrs. Dunne's shop was where the chemist's shop is now. She was a very friendly lady dressed all in black as older widowed ladies did then (as did shop assistants !) There was a long mahogany counter on one side of the shop, Mrs. Dunne sat behind it on a high chair presiding over the large till, chatting to customers and keeping a sharp eye on everything. I remember she always wore a magnificent cameo brooch at the neck of her dress and behind where she sat there was a red velvet curtain drawn to one side to reveal the staircase leading upstairs.

    Upstairs in the front room, Mrs. Dunne's daughter Anna taught piano lessons to local children. Anna had been a nun but when she contracted tuberculosis she had to leave the order and return home to live with her mother. I was one of her less talented pupils. Miss Dunne was a very strict teacher, who wrapped you sharply over the knuckles with her little cane should you make a mistake or play a wrong note ! I was not cut out to be a pianist, money and my mother's money could have been spent more profitably !

Occasionally during the teaching term, Miss Dunne would announce that there would be no class next week as her brother who worked in Waterford would be coming home for the weekend. It was a time for celebration for the family and a time of celebration too for this reluctant pupil !

So that's it, the famous Dunne's Stores of Dublin originally started life here in Rostrevor.

Miss Jean Baxter

"Mammy, Mammy ! Miss Baxter gave me a slap today !" That meant congratulations were in order; your child had achieved a reward for good work and this honour was not gained easily.

Miss Baxter had her own unique way of making her small charges learn how to work hard and to interact with other children courteously. A "slap" from Miss Baxter was a colouring book, delivered with a gentle tap on the outstretched hand of the child who had won the coveted prize for that week. On Fridays, at the end of class when the book was presented with great ceremony, Miss Baxter would relate the number of "stars" the lucky child had received for good work and any little acts of kindness she had noticed the child perform to others during the week. It was a great incentive for the small pupils to strive to do better next week and to behave, not a signal for parents to phone the authorities about child abuse !!!

For a few years "Biddy" Baxter, as she was known in schools, (behind her back of course !) taught English in Newry Intermediate School as it was known then, now Newry High School. There she was a strict and interesting teacher who instilled a love of poetry and drama in her pupils. She was responsible for the yearly talented drama productions in the school and many a would-be actor and actress learned from her tuition.

When my children started in the old two room Primary School in Rostrevor, Miss Baxter had charge of the juniors, Mr. Tom Roberts being the headmaster. There was a good relationship between them, although I really think the headmaster was a little in awe of her ! She was a formidable lady, not the prettiest, older and with a quiet air of authority that made me feel the need to go beyond the call of duty and collect more parental "stars" than needed ! In other words she scared me stiff !!

By now, she was living in a seaside cottage down a long lane beside Ballyedmond Estate and rode a bicycle with a little engine on it, to travel to Rostrevor every day. She always wore a big long mackintosh coat, yards of scarf and a sort of balaclava thing on her head as she putt-putted her way to school in all kinds of weather. Some years later she updated to a Lambretta scooter, again out in all weathers, never missing a class.

Miss Baxter looked fierce, didn't suffer fools gladly but underneath had a charming and kind nature, small children being her great delight, they loved her stories and company.

Each summer term, Miss Baxter would invite mothers and their children in her department to her Ballyedmond seaside home for afternoon tea, one family at a time. It was her way of getting to know parents and children out of the classroom. Her home was a lovely old stone cottage, very basic, no electricity, no phone, I'm not sure about the water supply or if she had a well.

I remember a big fireplace, beautiful antiques and paintings, comfortable sofas and oil lamps, the smell of well-polished furniture, big arrangements of garden flowers, books and more books, cats and more cats (only two were allowed inside). Miss Baxter lived alone and cats were her constant companions, treated like family and all had Shakespearean names like Hamlet, Juliet, Shylock and Romeo.

If the weather was nice and sunny, she loaded up a tray with sandwiches, lots of the favourite kind of buns and biscuits that children like, then tea and fruit juice was served in a sheltered corner of the garden. The children played on the grass with the friendliest cats or brought up treasure from the beach for Miss Baxter. She had a story that came alive for every bit of driftwood, shells, broken glass or pottery found, she was a remarkable lady.

Once when we were there, it started to rain and we had tea indoors. I was a nervous wreck because two of my boys were the inquisitive type and not used to having tea out of the finest bone china cups and saucers. One wanted to know why didn't she have good plastic mugs like we had at home ! Tactfully, Miss Baxter told him because for her, it was a special day to have two charming boys to tea and she thought that they were quite grown up enough to use nice china. They both sat up six inches taller ! To this day, two grown men speak fondly of Miss Baxter.

With just a year to go to her retirement, on a sunny

Easter Sunday morning, we heard the awful news that Miss Baxter and her elderly aunt who had been staying with her for a few days, had died in an early morning fire that completely destroyed her home. Kilbroney Primary School had lost a beloved teacher. Pupils who were lucky enough to have been taught by her learned not just academic lessons. Miss Baxter's "slap" never did anyone any harm !

Saturday Night Fever

Do you remember when the "second house" was showing on Saturday night ? We paid at the ticket office for the more expensive seats then walked up the carpeted stairs to the balcony, through the double doors into complete darkness and the sound from the adverts on the big screen would deafen you ! The usherette looked at your ticket and then proceeded to show you to your seat by the light from her torch through the fog of blue cigarette smoke ! Changed times in Kilkeel indeed.

One wet Saturday night, the latest John Wayne film was showing and needless to say the cinema was booked out. In the middle of the back row (a favourite place for courting couples) Jimmie and his new girlfriend Anne were on their first date.

Jimmie had booked the seats earlier that week hoping to pluck up the courage to ask Anne if she would come to the show with him. He did and she accepted ! Jimmie was a very nice guy, well reared, mannerly and handsome. His only drawback was that he always had trouble knowing his left hand from his right hand, maybe because he was ambidextrous.

Anyway, the big movie had just started when another couple arrived in late, causing the folks who were sitting in the first few seats in the row having to stand up, allowing the newcomers to pass to the two empty seats beside Jimmie and Anne. The newcomers settled down, whispering loudly to each other and immediately started on bags of crisps and sweets, not endearing themselves to their neighbours on either side.

The film was progressing to a tense moment and the audience were totally engrossed. Alone, out at the prairie homestead John Wayne on his horse, gun in hand was keeping the bad guys at bay, allowing the heroine to escape to safety. Jimmie slid his arm solicitously around Anne's waist, only to be met with another arm already securely there ! Jimmie had momently forgotten that Anne was seated on his right and had made a big mistake ! The other young man immediately jumped up from his seat to confront poor Jimmie, hitting him a thump on the face. Whereupon Jimmie, who was a member of the local boxing club, retaliated with vigour and blood started to flow.

The neighbours who were seated next and in the rows in front of the warring pair stood up, started shouting and swearing. Soon half the audience was involved, everyone objecting strongly to the interruption. The film was turned off and the lights went up. Management appeared, trying to control the situation, to no avail. Fist fights started in other parts of the auditorium, women started screaming and families began to make their way out of the melee.

Anne quickly picked up her handbag and joined the other escapees, hoping no-one would notice that she was involved with the troublemakers. She pretended not to hear the derogative comments being made by others in the crush to get out of the cinema and fled down the street to the bus terminal in time to catch a bus to Rostrevor and the safety of home ! Some people stopped long enough at the ticket office to demand their money back, others just fled out into the dark wet street !

Jimmie ? He took refuge in the back of the cleaner's broom cupboard until the management closed up the cinema for the night.

However, the disturbance didn't put the lovers off and three years ago they celebrated their Golden Wedding anniversary !

Killowen Village on Carlingford Lough

Joan and her father

At the post office or at the sign for the yacht club turn right. Fifty yards down the loanin turn right again, tucked well back from the strong gales and high tides, you'll come to a single row of ---- I suppose a dozen or so well-kept houses, known as the street. They were fishermen's cottages at one time and according to the old folk, there was a coastguard station there too. Yes, that's right, they are still there, all white paint, fancy windows, an aerial on every roof and two cars at the front door !! Ahh well, that's progress for you. Good luck to them, I say !

Let me take you back a few years. Then, every house had an outside toilet in the back yard and there was a pump at the end of the street for fresh water. Huh, couldn't you see families now having to carry buckets of water back to the house for everything ? Or getting water from the rain barrel at the back of the house and heat it up to wash their hair ? Or wash the children in a tin bath in front of the fire, having carried in the water and heated it up first ? Wouldn't they take a look at you ? No showers, no washing machines, no fridge freezers, no television, no computers, no central heating, no mobile phones, different lifestyle. Changed times indeed !

A laneway halfway down the street led to a triangular field, right on the edge of the shingly, sheltered bay. Wooden summer homes had been built there by families from Newry, Lurgan, Portadown, Armagh and faraway places like that, maybe twenty or thirty miles away. They were small, basic and well kept. The retired folk usually came first, around Easter at the start of the season, you know, probably to get a bit of maintenance done after the winter storms and have a bit of peace and quiet too. The weather could be nice then, but my goodness, when families came at the beginning of June and the school holidays started, the place was coming down with youngsters ! It was great !

My Dad had built one of these small wooden houses there too, with the idea of renting it out to visitors for the summer months but somehow that plan was changed. Our family moved down to Killowen Point and our house which was about a mile away, up on the main Kilkeel road was rented out instead ! ---- Lucky us !! The Kellys, the

Bloomfields, Murphys, McCavanas, Donnellys, Erskines, Manneys, Maguires, Kennedys, O'Hares, Murphy cousins galore and sure that's only the half of them who lived there for the Summer, playing every rain or shine day on Killowen beach !

    In my childhood, the early war years, the O'Neills lived next door to the wee pink cottage on the corner of the street. They kept a cow or two in the field at the back and sold milk ------ not in cartons or glass bottles, you had to bring your own jug or tin can. Up at the post office on the main road, Mrs. Savage, the postmistress sold stamps, envelopes, postal orders, sweets, cigarettes, minerals, fresh eggs from a big wicker basket, sent telegrams or helped you make a telephone call from a big black trumpet thing, high up on the wall in her little office. The post office was in the front room of the roadside farmhouse where Mrs. Savage lived.

    Every Friday, old McVeigh came with his horse and cart, flies dividing their time between the horse and the cargo of lovely fresh herrings from Kilkeel. The horse would patiently wait, flicking his mane now and then at the annoying flies, while the women customers (with their plates for the fish) had their chat with Barney. Oh yes, I nearly forgot, Inglis's red bread van came twice a week with the bread ----- I can smell it yet ! Big batch loaves with the crusty top, Paris buns, sugar tops and currant squares (which we called flies cemeteries !) On the other days, Hughes bread van called with lovely soda bread and potato bread. Mind you, several of the mammies made bread and big pots of soup every day ------ we didn't go hungry !

Some of the fathers usually travelled to work, often sharing lifts, in cars that needed cranked up or pushed to get started in the morning. Remember this was wartime, petrol was rationed, the bus was often late and the train only came to Warrenpoint five miles away. The mammies were left all day with nothing to do (we thought) but look after the kids, feed us and have a wee gossip with each other !

Due to their work, some daddies stayed at home all week and only came down at the weekend bringing goodies from home and sometimes, Granny !! It's funny how some Grannies were great fun, even if they were old and others you never went near at all, if you could help it !

The local children who lived in the street or nearby, got on well with the "summer folk". Each year games between them continued, as if Winter had never happened. Games like rounders (Killowen version), sardines, cock of Russia, tenniquoits, (anyone else ever heard of it ?) cricket (again the Killowen version !) The rough grass in front of the houses across the laneway, just yards from the beach was our playground. Adults spent hours cutting hedges and grass around their houses. They puttied leaky windows, they tarred leaky felt roofs and minded leaky babies. They grew good spuds, hard tomatoes, wormy radishes and rescued lettuce from the snails. They all grew tanned and fit in the fresh air and sea breeze.

If it turned out a wet evening, there'd be a card game of whist or canasta in somebody's house, otherwise, on a fine evening the adults would gather at the old summer seat under the two pine trees, after they had the children settled in bed, for a bit of craic and a singsong.

(Just noted, in my lifetime the two pine trees, summer seat, the last small house and half the stone wall have disappeared ----- winter storms, erosion or climate change ?)

Sometimes there'd be a concert in farmer Houston's barn, at the other end of the street, that would be a great night. The barn was cleared of all the bags of potatoes and farm equipment. Planks of wood were set up on blocks, to make rows of seats. War time black out, so the window and door had to be covered with old bags, to make sure not a glimmer of light from the Tilley lamps could be seen from outside by any of Hitler's boys, should they fly over Carlingford Lough ! A stage was set up, decorated with old curtains and the excited audience filled the barn.

One of the men did "master of ceremonies" and he always had some smart stories to keep people laughing, before introducing the artists which we all knew well ! Some of the parents did a turn and so did most of the children ------ at least the show-offs who went to elocution classes or Irish dancing did ! Some of the children sniggered, others were embarrassed when Mammy or Daddy got up on the makeshift stage. Mr. Kelly from Newry sang "The Rose of Tralee" far better than Count John McCormack, so everybody said. Joe and Mrs. Mac played the banjo and accordion. Everyone clapped and sang "She'll be coming round the mountain when she comes" and "The boys from the County Armagh" ----- Wee Joe could fairly make that banjo talk, so he could. Miss O'Neill had a wonderful contralto voice, she could be heard two fields away ! Mrs. Bloomfield, she of the Operatic Society, was terrifying when she sang "There's a hole in the bucket", with her husband Tommy, who always took his teeth out to sing the part of stupid auld Henry, much to our delight !

Ahh dear me, many's a good laugh we had. Now that I think of it, I wonder why their children were never in the audience to see them sing --- we always had to tell them that they had just missed it. Davy Boyd told stories of the wee folk, changeling babies and the banshee. Many's an unruly child crept closer to their Mammy as the spooky stories went on and on. Sometimes, there'd be a magician who had us all baffled. Just how did he cut Mrs. Daly in half and why did Mr. Daly not jump up to save her ?!

After that it would be time for supper. Strong tea, tomato and egg sandwiches, fancy buns, scones and jam, stuff in black bottles at the back of the barn for some of the men, lemonade or creamola for the children. The air was thick with smoke from the Gallaher's, Woodbine and plug pipe tobacco but sure, nobody minded at all ------- we knew no different.

When the singsong was over, about eleven o'clock,

the mammies gathered up their sleepy heads and took them off home to bed. The men stayed on, dismantled all the temporary seating and platform, carried back in the bags of spuds, machines and left Issac's barn in order. They stayed on a while, smoked, yarned and discussed the "Hitler problem" till dawn.

All during the Summer, families of seals lived and played on the rocks, away out beyond farmer Houston's barn. They swam, fished and reared their young, echoing life with the summer folk on shore.

Food rationing was on but supplies of white flour, (most families made their own bread and cakes) cooked ham, butter, tea and those special Hafner's sausages were never a problem. You see, some of the men had business interests over the border in the South. People were generous and shared with each other ------ besides, Carlingford was only a short boat trip across the Lough. Easy enough to avoid the customs officers or the Home Guard but sure that's a story for another day !

The war was a long way off and the worst that could happen was four wet days in a row, no drying outside and a houseful of yappy small kids ! Parents got together to listen to the nine o'clock news from the BBC or the ten o'clock news from Radio Eireann on the wireless and well dare any child not yet in bed squeak ! They followed the Allies progress through Europe, the D-day landings, worried about bombing on the English cities, fiddled with low batteries, dry batteries and noisy interference, to hear the latest bit of information or the propaganda from Lord Haw-Haw. Anyway, the war progressed without the advice of the Killowen Point residents !

Some empty houses around the street and beyond were requisitioned by the authorities and rented to families from Belfast, in case the Germans bombed the city. It was the same all over the North and I'm sure the thought of living in an out of the way place like Killowen caused distress and heartache to the evacuees. To the locals and migratory residents it caused interest and alarm, fear and admiration, something to blame if things went wrong ! Suddenly the war seemed a lot closer.

Local children and the evacuees had an uneasy tolerance of each other and natural leaders began to emerge in both camps. At first adults were polite and hospitable but soon attitudes changed. Parents blamed the newcomers for being a bad influence. City kids were so outspoken, advanced and didn't take no for an answer. Adult newcomers were a bit too cocky, smart, didn't understand country life and were too sure of themselves ----- "They're worth a'watching, you'd need to mind them boys !" Another thing about them, they'd no respect for the sea, the nearby mountains or the weather for that matter ----- "Ahh, they'll get their comeuppance alright !!"

Most of the children spent the day on the beach, in and out of the water, chasing each other, shouting and screeching, having fun. There was an old raft and a couple of oars that some of the fathers had procured for them. It was tethered to the shore by a long length of chain, so that it could not drift out to sea. The big boys loved to push it out quickly, so that it would jerk when it reached the end of the chain and everyone would fall in ! Miracle that none of the youngsters were drowned, that was the way we learned to swim ! Miracle none of us drowned, health and safety it was not !!

Usually, some of the older folk around would notice if something was wrong. Locals and the summer children were mostly good swimmers and knew the dangers. The evacuee children were smart, learned quickly to swim and took risks.

One of the older evacuee lads had a "gra" as we would say, for pretty girls. The youngest daughter of one of the summer families fell for his city slicker patter and style. One day, he was trying to impress her by supervising the young swimmers. After a while, he forgot his duties and was sweet talking her behind the rocks, when a small child got into difficulties in the water. The other children, splashing and pushing each other in fun, didn't realise what was happening. One of the older local boys did notice and managed to grab the little one as she floated past on the ebb tide. The child soon recovered and no harm was done but the talk went round about the evacuee's carelessness. That put a hasty end to the romance, after her Daddy chased him with a pitchfork when he saw the lad hanging round their gateway !

All the while, the seals and their pups were watching and playing on the big rocks, echoing the family life on shore. The night the Germans bombed Belfast, panic-stricken families listened to the drone of the engines overhead and knew their city was the target. Wave after wave of them passed behind the broken cloud, carrying their deadly cargo. Towards dawn, some of the Belfast men climbed Slieve Martin, the big mountain behind the village. They saw the angry red sky and knew their city was burning. Their families were safe but what of their relations and friends ?

By now, the evacuee children felt confident enough to challenge the locals to a diving competition at the big rocks. The children had been told not to swim on their own because of the near-tragedy some time before but supervision was the last thing these young ones wanted. The word "teenager" hadn't been invented then. Secretly, word went around to meet at the big rocks at high tide but high tide that night was not until 3 am. Parents wondered why it was so easy to get the young ones to bed that bright summer's evening. Later, when everyone was asleep, the girls smuggled out milk, lemonade and biscuits. They brought old towels and dry clothes, stuffed pillows down their beds and stole quietly out from their homes and headed for the big rocks. The boys were already there and raring to go. The boys dived and dived again, again and again.

One of the big girls had brought her father's stopwatch and she knew how to use it ! She timed the seconds spent underwater by each diver. The newcomers seemed to be winning and the locals were getting anxious. Two of the younger boys agreed to dive again. The girl with the stopwatch held her breath, couldn't believe the length of time before the first head appeared and then further out glimpsed the second head, she declared him the winner ! The evacuees had won by a whisker ! Everyone slapped each other and jumped for joy. The local boy came out of the water to get dried but where did the winner get to ? Where did he go ? He just wasn't there ! Could it have been a seal they saw ? His friends said he'd be fine ----- Sure wasn't he a great wee swimmer, the best ? He'd be playing a joke on them, maybe hiding behind a rock. Maybe he thought he'd let the side down ---- No, no, he'll come up OK in Carlingford or Greencastle and walk it home ------ just wait and see ! He'll be OK. The rest gathered up the remains of the picnic and headed for home, talking quietly among themselves. Did he really stay down all that time ? Did he run away ? However, they made a pact to say nothing and crept home to bed.

    The boy's parents became alarmed when he did not appear the next day. It was not unusual for children to stay over or eat at friend's houses. Children had freedom those days unheard of in this day. There was always pots of soup, bread and wee buns on the go and mammies fed any child who turned up at meal times, no questions asked. The kids denied all knowledge of him. Police, parents, Home Guard and the priest were called, all combed the area for him and found nothing. The family decided that he had tried to make his own way back to Belfast. He had been so worried about his Granda, Granny and Toby, their pet dog, in those awful air raids that they had heard about. That was it, he'd be OK. He'd turn up in a day or two, just say a wee prayer for him. Surely somebody would see a wee black-haired fellow on his own ?

Funny thing though, it was about then that the seal pup started coming ashore every morning for a little while, just in front of the houses. The boy's younger brother used to go down to the beach after his breakfast to talk to the young seal and bring it a bit of toast ---- his brother always loved toast and jam !

Now how's that for a real story ? And no, they never did find a body.

Mrs. McNeice's School

Autumn again and the new school year was already well underway. Our wee school was typical of many in those far off days. It was privately owned by a well-qualified teacher, Mrs. McNeice who taught small children from the area in her own home, before they went to the big public elementary school.

Mrs. McNeice was a large lady, at least she seemed very large to my small six-year old self, whom we called Martha Minnie behind her back. Martha Minnie was a formidable lady with high Christian values and even higher principles. No, you didn't "mess" with Martha Minnie, as they say nowadays.

The McNeices lived in the last terrace house in Killowen Village, with Joey O'Neill's big field right next to it on the other side. Mr. McNeice was a retired farmer and I always remember him with a spade digging vegetables in his large garden or washing potatoes in a bucket under an outside tap in his yard, although I'm sure he had other duties too !

The one large schoolroom, or classroom as we called it, was at the back of the house, one window looked out on to Joey's field, the classroom door and another window opened out to the yard and garden which was quite big. There was a large grassy area with an old apple tree in the middle of it, so there was plenty of room for the nine or ten small pupils to play in at break time. The small wooden hut at the other side of the garden, with the red corrugated tin roof was the dry toilet. Those of you who have never heard of a "dry toilet" ----- ask your Granny !! There were usually some creepy crawleys on the cement floor as the door did not quite touch the ground, making the necessary trips there (at least in my case) as quick as possible. The walls were whitewashed and well disinfected, to this day the smell of Jeyes Fluid always reminds me of it !

    The big apple tree was an early fruiting variety, small red and stripy. In early September they were nearly past their best and any windfalls on the ground were usually crawling with wasps (in spite of Mr. McNeice brushing them up every morning !) Mrs. McNeice always warned us to be careful and not to pick any up. They were very sweet, a great temptation to small children as this was during wartime and sweets were a luxury.

    To this day, I remember the shame and disgrace of being caught by Mrs. McNeice when the two small apples that I had stolen rolled out from where I had hidden them and rolled across the floor of the classroom. Little girls in those days wore knickers with a pocket on one side for your hankie ----- IMAGINE !! The wrath of God had nothing on the wrath of Mrs. McNeice towards the wrongdoer ! Apples ? No thanks !! I learned my lesson. Gaining her forgiveness was another lesson.

The classroom had four or five desks and a big table covered with books, the teacher's chair placed behind it. There was a glass-fronted wooden press in the corner where all our books were kept neatly beside the pile of Vere Foster exercise books. On the top shelf, a large stone jar of Stephen's Ink sat beside boxes of new pencils and pens with nibs, the big round-faced school clock was high on the wall just to the left. I remember that one of the older boys had the important job of carefully filling the ink wells on the desks every morning. Vere Foster exercise books had words and sayings written in perfect copperplate script and we had to copy them time and time again until perfect for Mrs. McNeice's approval.

The walls were covered with maps of the world and the British Empire, missionaries bringing God's Word to people in foreign lands and looking after their babies if their Mammy died. Oh yes, there were pictures of our native trees and birds but none of the children's work was displayed, as far as I can remember, although we were well praised for good work. The one small window looked out into Joey's field and there were usually a few bullocks grazing there. Sometimes they would come right up to the window and look in at us and sometimes Mrs. McNeice would have to close the window in a hurry if there was a bad smell just outside !

When Martha Minnie called you up to stand beside her to read, recite poetry or rhyme off the tables learnt for homework she gave each child her undivided attention and the rest of us knew better than to talk. My mother kept the school reports she sent home at the end of term and in later years I was surprised to see that we were taught some basic French, art, maths and English at such an early age.

Mrs. McNeice did her best to educate and encourage us to have inquiring minds and for that I thank her and for the memories of gentler days.

Wait Te You Hear This One !

My Granny could hear and see the Banshee, and not everybody can say that ! She could scare the livin' daylights out of us children. She'd come in through the back door, shake the rain of her coat, hang it up on the peg and come on into the kitchen. Normally she'd call out her usual cheery greeting and give off about the weather but if it was a dark wet day when she visited we sort of knew what was coming. After the hugs and kisses she'd nod her head, look at us solemnly and start.

"Yestery evening I was just comin' up the loanin and I heerd ------". We'd all look at each other and pretend to be getting on with our homework. Mammy would raise her eyes heavenward, heave a big sigh and get on with whatever household chore she happened to be doing. "Nana, I think maybe you heard the ambulance in the distance. I'll put the kettle on, a wee cup of tea would be nice and then you can tell us what you have been up to this week. Have you been shopping or doing a bit in the garden ? Any more word from Auntie Mary ?"

Mammy had always a good way of changing the subject if she thought things weren't suitable for our ears. We scribbled away and waited for the home-made buns or cake which we knew Nana would take out from the big bag she always carried. When the tea was poured and the lovely fresh buns devoured Nana began her story all over again.

"I started to tell you, Kathleen and then it went clean out of my mind ------". Always the same beginning. We stared at her, willing her to tell us the scary bits before Mammy chased us off to do something else. Once Nana started, she was like a river in full flood. The words just tumbled out, then a pause to let that bit of the story sink in, before another torrent started.

You know when a river is in flood churning up white water, the way a bit of a branch can get caught up and has to rest before the rush of water frees it and it takes off again ? Well, that reminds me of my Nana's stories. The wee rest gives you time to try to work out what she has just told you. The only thing is she knows too many people that we don't know and she goes into far too much detail. They all seem to be related or married to somebody that is related to some distant cousin of somebody else that were the neighbours donkeys' years ago. Very hard to work that out.

Mammy just nods in agreement but after a while you can see that she has lost the thread of the story. She glances at the clock a lot or looks out of the window. Sometimes she contradicts Nana as to who the people were married to or where they lived. I thought it was very bad manners to contradict older people, specially your mother or father. Well, so WE were always told !! There you are now, grown-ups are not always consistent !

"As I was saying, Kathleen, I was coming up the loanin yestery evening. It was just starting to draw in, I was thinking the long dark nights are coming soon and it will be time to get the fire lit. When you are on your own there's nothing like a good fire to keep you company, you have to tend it, sure it's nearly as much trouble as a husband !! Then I remembered that I had put washing on the line earlier, there was good dryin' yestery d'ye mind. So I had to go round the back of the house to the garden to bring them in but first I had to go into the house to get the -----". (Please, please, PLEASE Nana, just get on with it, leave the washing out ----- I promise it's not going to rain tonight, no matter what you think !) "----- basket. Then I saw it ! I couldn't believe what it was. No, it definitely should NOT have been there this time of year. It was just beside a stone on the path, in front of the hedge and I wasn't imagining it. I thought it was just the evenin' light glintin' on something. It looked like a wee snowdrop but sure, what would a wee snowdrop be doing on the path at the end of September ? Och, the auld head's away with it ! I looked again and as sure as the good Lord made wee green apples, it winked at me !!"

Mammy, by this time was wondering what she was going to make for dinner before Daddy came home from work. We were pop-eyed, for we knew there was more, much more to come and we hoped the "auld Divil" would come into it somehow. "The wee snowdrop winked at Nana, Mammy !" my younger sister squealed.

"I got the basket and headed off over the grass to the clothes-line, as quick as the sore feet would let me. I was just taking the pegs off the first towel when a big black jackdaw swooped down and perched on the end of the line. 'Mrs. McCann, I have a wee message for you.' ----- Heavens, it was the jackdaw talkin' to me ! And before I could say a word he flew off. 'Ach, you're getting old' I said to myself. 'Jackdaws talking, would ye wise up !'"

We looked at each other. Nana ALWAYS told the truth. "Tell the truth and shame the Devil", she always told us ---- no matter what. Anyway, how could a jackdaw talk ? Tell the truth and shame the Devil.

"I put the clothes into the basket and headed up the path to the back door, as if nothing had happened when I heard this awful screechin' and keenin'. It seemed to be coming from a long way off, somewhere away up behind the trees at the top of Martin's Hill. My heart was thumpin', for I knew what it was ! The wailing and keenin' went on and on. I stopped short, the sweat broke on me, me hairs stood on end and not a bone in my body would move ! I was stuck to the ground, so I just said a wee prayer to our good Lord to keep us all safe. It was the Banshee herself who had a message for me !!"

I looked at Mammy, who was holding wee Jimmie's hand and then Sharon (who was only five) climbed up on her knee and cuddled in. I knew that Nana didn't joke about these things, for she had come from a long line (so she always told us) of ancestors where one in every generation had the "gift" of second sight and the gift had been handed down to her. The Banshee, the old woman of Irish mythology was a friend of my Granny ------ how cool is that !! But the good Lord is also her friend and she often told us how He would always, ALWAYS look after us all, we just had to trust in Him.

"Then there was a loud swooshing noise and something bluey-black swished past my head and settled in the big apple tree. Kathleen, I was scared stiff, for she never came that close to me before, although I've heard her many's a time. I thought she was goin' to warn me about somebody I know who was about to die or tell me that my time's up but the keenin' and cryin' just went on and on !! What do you think she meant ?"

Mammy sighed, got up and looked out of the window. "Nana, I'm not saying there's no such thing as the Banshee but I'd be very surprised if it was her because it wasn't that dark and there wasn't a full moon. Over at the next farm, Jimmy Quinn has been cutting down some trees these past few days and you know the whine that chainsaws make can carry a long way on a still evening. I've been watching big flocks of swallows and house martins swooping about lately. I suppose they are busy, gathering up for their long journey south for the Winter. Nana, I've put a big casserole in the oven, will you stay and have dinner with us, won't you ? Peter will be home soon and sure, we'll leave you home later."

Trust Mammy to spoil a good story !

Portadown, Here We Come !

Our Aunt Norah was great fun. The sun always shone in Lurgan in those days when we stayed with her and Uncle Walter for our annual holiday. It must have been July or August when our misadventure happened, it doesn't really matter because every day was full of surprises, adventure and excitement for two small girls.

Auntie Norah's surprises were something else ! It could be a big potato under your pillow, instead of your pyjamas or maybe a packet of Rollo sweets stuck down your shoe when you couldn't get your foot into it ! You just didn't know what to expect next but it was always fun. Uncle Walter was a big jovial pipe-smoking man and, as long as his dinner was on the table when he came home from work, he was happy to tell us funny stories while letting Auntie Norah enjoy the excitement of shopping with the two wee nieces.

Lurgan was so different from Killowen where we lived. There were rows of shops in different streets and they sold different things in each one ! Not like our one shop that sold everything. There was a big park with a lake in the middle of it, where Auntie Norah would take us every day to feed the lovely ducks with the stale bread that we had brought with us. Best of all, there was a special place for children to play in, with two sets of swings; small ones for small children and larger ones for bigger children ! We always made a beeline for the big ones if there were no other children about. Auntie

Norah never shouted at us to mind this or that, not that our mother was cross ----- but she always seemed to be warning us about something when we were out playing !

Auntie Norah loved shopping and knew most of the staff in every shop. Getting us dressed up to walk us up town was her great joy. Of course we were on show, paraded in and out of shops, so that everyone could see how much we had grown since last year and comment on the family likeness between my wee sister and her ! While she talked to the ladies behind the counters and made her purchases, we were free to look around but not touch anything in these "Aladdin's caves".

When our aunt was paying for her purchases at the counter of one particular shop, they had these funny wooden balls that came apart, the lady put money inside, closed it up again and off it went, whizzing up a wee railway track thing to the office upstairs ! Pure magic !! Then there'd be a ding-ding noise, it whizzed back down to the counter, the lady would open it and give Auntie her change and receipt. We used to stand waiting for another customer to pay her bill !! Oh, the excitement of it ! You certainly wouldn't see that in Killowen.

Auntie Norah and Uncle Walter had important friends who lived in Portadown and we were invited there for afternoon tea. Uncle Walter couldn't (or perhaps didn't) want to go, so it was planned that Auntie Norah would take us there by train.

That morning, our best dresses were ironed, shoes polished, clean white socks and underwear left out for us. Hair was washed with Auntie Norah's special shampoo (for blonds), rinsed with a little vinegar in warm water (for a good shine) and brushed dry in the warm sunshine. The early lunch over, we were dressed in our pretty white trobalco dresses with the coloured dots and our gleaming hair tied up with matching ribbons. Auntie Norah suitably attired, proud as a peacock, walked us up town towards the railway station.

As I told you, she knew lots of people and a walk with her meant lots of stopping to chat. It also meant lots of hopping around on one leg or looking for "lost treasure" in the gutter, like cigarette butts or snails, while we stood by, waiting for the adults to finish their conversation. Today was different ----- we had a train to catch ! It's quite a long walk for small legs from one end of Lurgan to the other but we had plenty of time to get to the station, even allowing for ladies to admire the beautiful little nieces !

Lurgan railway station was a big noisy place, especially for a pair who had never been there before or even seen a train close up. We stood very close to our aunt and took in all the sights and sounds. A train arrived at the opposite platform, stopped with a loud screech and swishes of steam. People got out of carriages, doors banged, someone blew a loud whistle and the train puffed gently away. We watched it all. The people climbed the wooden stairs, crossed over the bridge, down the stairs on our side and went out of the big doors beside us.

Auntie Nora had assured us that our train was not due yet and we were to stay well away from the edge of the platform. She had found a seat and was happily chatting away with two ladies. Another train came in, more people got off, more swishes of hot air, more doors banged, people disappeared, a man in uniform kept blowing a whistle and the train moved slowly away out of the station.

By now my sister and I had got the hang of this platform thing. Auntie Norah was still chatting to the ladies and so long as we didn't venture too far away, she was quite happy. We saw a train coming and knew it wasn't the one for Portadown. We thought if we went up the stairs to the bridge we could get a better look at the train below. We could and we did ! We watched the train puff off slowly below us and made our way back to our aunt.

Auntie Norah took one look at us and gave a loud scream ! She said a word we knew was VERY bad !! I looked at my sister, she was all black and sooty ----- her face, arms and the white dress was no longer white but she was all smiles. "Auntie Norah, Auntie Norah ----- guess what ? The man in the engine waved his hand at me !"

My arms and legs were the same ----- mostly black, even the wee coloured dots on my dress were, well, a bit sooty ! Auntie Norah rushed us to the "Ladies Rest Room" but even with her hankie dipped into water she knew it was hopeless to try and clean us. She kept us there until she was sure that the train for Portadown had left, then with eyes averted, marched us swiftly home to the other end of Lurgan and never stopped once to bid anyone the time of day !

    After the big clean up and the apologies were written (no handy mobile phones then) to her posh friends, we heard Uncle Walter laugh and say something about pride and a fall. ------ We didn't know what he was talking about, sure we didn't fall !!

Family Years

The Fortune Teller: The Big Night Out

Invitations for the autumn wedding were already posted. There were lacy trousseau things in a suitcase on the bed in the spare room. It was a dirty wet Friday night in Summer many years ago and the girls had called for me in Kathleen's father's big car.

Kathleen thought she was a good driver, we did too because she had driven to Belfast with her father and he didn't have to shout at her once. This was in the days before the dreaded national driving test and fathers were the usual instructors for new drivers.

The car was full of laughter and Elvis was at full blast on the radio ----- Or maybe it was Dean ? It didn't matter ! We were off on a girlie night out, decked "to the nines" in the latest fashion and reeking of Elizabeth Arden perfume. Come October I would be the first to break our circle, things just wouldn't be the same and we knew it. Tonight was going to be special, tonight we were off to visit the famous Joe in Newcastle. Joe was a fortune teller, known far and wide for his predictions.

The other two had boyfriends, sometimes subject to change, but I had a wonderful man, a lovely engagement ring and a big do coming up soon. Near Annalong there was a shriek from June in the back, reminding us that we had forgotten the tea and biscuits !! June had been to fortune tellers before and knew the ropes. No money changed hands but a gift of foodstuffs or something was acceptable before "yer man" would let us over his door and we hadn't anything with us. Kathleen pulled up at the first wee shop we saw ----- we still had lots of them through the country back then. June and I jumped out into the pouring rain and made a dash for the door, the bell jangled, the smell of paraffin oil was overpowering but we were in and dry ! June bought the ciggies, sweets and as an after-thought, tea and biscuits.

"So yez are off to see Joe, are you ?" asked the auld man behind the counter. "No, indeed we are not !" I answered, with all the dignity I could muster. "We are going to have a picnic." (Any fool would know that only girls with not much hope would visit a fortune teller to find out if there was anything on the horizon at all ----- I wasn't stupid !) He raised one eyebrow, glanced out at the rain and said, "You'll be needing milk and sugar no doubt. And what about paraffin and matches for the Primus ?"

The bill came to a lot more than we expected and we rustled up the cash between us. After all, we couldn't ask Kathleen for money, she was our driver and transport. I knew he didn't believe the picnic thing for one second ------- nosey old bugger !! Anyway, it was "Goodnight Mister" and out to the car with the goodies. We opened the car windows to clear the mist, started on the ciggies and vowed never to call there again.

Newcastle was still a good fifteen minutes away at our

speed and Kathleen knew that Joe lived in a cottage on the right-hand side going out of Newcastle. We tried the Kilkeel road, the Castlewellan road, the Dundrum road, the Bryansford road, then gave up and went to the Strand for an ice-cream. It was still only eight o'clock, so we thought we should have another go at it. Along the road we saw a heavily waterproofed couple walking their dog. Kathleen slowed down beside them and asked where the fortune teller lived. "Just round the next corner, it's the house with all the cars at it ----- you'd think there was a wake. I wish I was going with you girls for the craic !" said the old lady with a smile. "Sure it would beat walking the dog with 'him' in the rain any night ! Have a good time." The husband waved us on and shouted after us that women didn't appreciate a good man when they had one. We didn't take the time to explain that we weren't looking for a man, only to get an idea of how things might turn out !!

At the next fork in the road cars were parked on both sides. Wee cars, big cars, old vans, some up on the narrow footpath, others halfway up the ditch. There seemed to be people in some of them. Where on earth did they all come from on a bucketing wet night like this ? Kathleen got out and interviewed a couple in the car in front. She came back with the news that we would have to wait a while but Joe never turned anyone away. On busy nights, he didn't waste time with too much chat, you were in and out in no time at all. Out came the ciggies and the windows were rolled down again. Elvis was still helping Radio Luxembourg with their ratings and we were having a good time. Girls and women came down the road in dribs and drabs, got into waiting cars and drove off. Men were few and far between. There were shrieks and giggles from some of the women but others stood in huddles talking quietly. "Looks a bit like bad news after the exams" June remarked.

Eventually, it looked like we were next in line. Do we give him the tea and biscuits when we go in or do we wait till we are leaving ? What if we should have brought coffee and chocolates or cooked ham and eggs ? Off we splashed down the little path to the door. The big man met us at the door with a wide smile. "Just go into the parlour there and I'll be with youse in a minute."

Orders are orders so in we went and sat down like three good wee girls in the small, dark over-crowded front room. Joe came back with three cups of doubtful cleanliness, full of well stewed black tea. "It takes the tay to be good and strong, otherwise the leaves won't stick and give you a good reading. Youse ones would like things to be right, I think." "OK OK, Joe, you're right but how am I going to drink this stuff ?" I thought, having a wee panic; I couldn't look at the other two. Good host that he was, our comfort was his concern. "I'll just go and get a lock of sticks for the fire, that auld damp gets into ye, sure it's no Summer at all, and then we'll get started" a big hearty laugh and with that he was away.

I looked around wildly for somewhere to dump the tea or at least some of it ! I needed to save some of the leaves at the bottom of the cup, otherwise Joe wouldn't be able to tell me how many children I would have and how successful they would be when they grew up, or of the beautiful mansion we would live in; with nine bedrooms, six bathrooms and a big swimming pool.

Kathleen was sitting on a hard upright chair with her back to the window and the window sill was full of overgrown geraniums in old pots. I stood up, intending to pour some of the black brew into the biggest pot and at that moment Kathleen had the same idea ! We both hit the unfortunate geranium with an avalanche of hot tea at the same time !! The plants hadn't been watered for many a day and the hard-baked soil was in no fit state to cope with so much liquid. I moved my chair closer to hers to block the view of the flowers.

Joe arrived back with an armful of sticks and soon a cheery blaze lit up the room. "Right, girls ----- who's first ? The girl with the nice dark hair, your name's June ?" He was a right old charmer ! June heard all the things she wanted to and more. All about the well-paid job that would turn up within the space of three, could be three weeks or three months or maybe three years. Funny thing was, she was starting a new job in Rathfriland on Monday and it was Friday ----- THREE DAYS !! Old Joe knew a thing or two !!

Kathleen was next. Her highlight was the news that a wealthy man who worked in Canada but who originally came from Newry (with the initial G in his name) was besotted with her and she would hear from him soon.

My turn at last, I had carefully hidden my ring before I came in. Joe studied the dregs in my cup and eyed me up and down. "Well my girl, if you haven't already got a ring, you'll soon be getting one but don't let it worry you, for you'll never marry him anyway ! He's not the one for you, that's all I can tell you. Goodnight ! Oh, by the way are you going on a holiday ? I see a half-packed suitcase here."

With that bit of news, the tea started to drip from the cracked plant pot onto the lino floor ! We couldn't wait to get out. June said it was hard to make out which end of me it was coming from ------ Always good for a laugh, our June but I couldn't laugh if I tried ! What on earth was I going to tell my mother ? After all the hard work, worry and expense she had preparing for this wedding, the first in our family. Oh, the shame of it ! And me practically a married woman !

We walked back to the car, the girls trying to keep my spirits up. They were tactful, not mentioning the news that Joe had given them and I knew that they were sad about missing a good day out at the wedding. We stopped at the chippy on the way home but even the chips seemed sodden. Oh, the worry of it ! I should have had a bit of wit, I should have waited for them in the car ! What will the husband-to-be think of me ? All my fault !! Well, the long and the short of it was ------ we never let on ! Good friends are like that, they'll stick with you when you need them, in good times and bad.

Anyway, coming down the aisle I saw them giving us the thumbs up. Fifty good years have since passed and I've warned the grandchildren to watch out for fortune tellers ! They're not ALWAYS right, you know !!

The Fortune Teller: The Housekeeper

I'm Sally McKevitt, Miss by choice ye know. M'family lived down at the fork of the road, just past the bad bend. Da worked on the roads for the council and Mam looked after the lot of us. There wasn't much left in the purse of a Saturday night I can tell ye ! Howaniver, we did alright. I left school at fourteen for I had no interest in the learnin'. M'mother was at her wits end for our auld targe of a teacher was always complainin' about me and she had enough to worry about, God love her !

    The Maguires lived in the big grey house at the top of the hill, ye know, the one in the trees behind the high wall. Just him and her and the four childer. He was what ye'd call a gentleman farmer, more gentleman than farmer I'd say ! Very edjicated and fond of his books. Och now, he wasn't that fond of the work but he was one very dacent, civil wee man.

    Anyway, one day Mrs. Maguire asked Mam if she knew of any strong young girl that would give her a hand with the childer, do a bit of cleanin', willin' to learn and earn a few shillin's a week. Mam wasn't long about gettin' me fixed up, whether I wanted to or not. That's what happened in them days ----- ye did what ye were toul. Aye, and I have no regrets for it was the makin' of me. I helped rear them young ones and they all did well, so they did. I lived in with them, I had me own wee room and all. It was lovely for we slept three in a bed at home !

The Missus taught me good plain cookin', how to keep the house spotless and how to boil the whites till they were like snow. She come from good stock at the other end of the County, you know. Indeed, the boss was a fine man too, straight as a dye and he was well thought of in the country about here, I couldn't say a bad word about him. It was a sad day when he tuk bad and died the very next day. The auld heart just gave up ----- Lord have mercy on him.

"Sally, ye can't leave us now," she said. She knew I had a hankerin' to go to Liverpool to our Bridie. Bridie was a good bit older than me, and married to a nice fella from Mayobridge, he worked on the railway over there ----- Aye, she did well for herself but I stayed on and one by one the childer all went off ----- England, America, New Zealand ----- Sure I couldn't leave the Missus all on her own in that big house.

It was soon after that we got the notion of keepin' lodgers, for there was plenty of spare rooms and money was not plentiful after the boss died. It's a great area round here for the fishin' and there's only the one wee hotel in the village. Mr. Brown runs the hotel and he asked the Missus if she would consider takin' in a couple of respectable fishermen now and then if he was overbooked at times. Old Mrs. Larkin used to do it for him for years but she had to give it up when she went to live with her daughter. The Missus was keen to give it a go but YOU-KNOW-WHO had all the work to do !! Och sure, it would keep me out of mischief and give us something to talk about !

Our ones had mostly died off and Charlie had got the home place, such as it was. He got the grant and the water and electricity laid on and you wouldn't know the place. He married a right wee beesom but sure, if she does him she'll do me, she keeps the place well ------ I'll give her that !! Well now I had niver married, sure I niver had the time ----- or the inclination, as they say ! True enough, there was one or two who looked my way but niver the right one. Auld scaldy Jimmy Mac, who hadn't tuppence or let on he hadn't, was one and I can't mind who the other was. I couldn't be bothered or maybe I was hard to please. Och, with one thing and another ------ too busy spring cleanin', too busy makin' jam, or too busy gettin' the garden tied up.

Now, one of the fishermen who stayed with us every so often was very ------ what'll I say ? Och, he was gettin' far too familiar and he made me uncomfortable with his auld talk. He was a nice enough man, very polite ----- but I don't think I could have stomached him for any length of time. Tell you the truth he was what I'd call an "auld Jinny" !! The Missus used to pull me leg about him all the time, "Well Sally, you could do a lot worse. He's no hangers on, no family and he's not short of money !" she'd say, and I'd tell her to run away on there and not put a good thing past herself !! Oh, we had great craic together but I knew my place.

The Missus always said that this house couldn't run

without me and the fishermen would have no place to go. The food they got at the hotel wasn't a patch on the grub I set up for them and well they knew it !

She always said the childer would never come back, for they all had good jobs and it was too quiet here for them. Now, she didn't exactly say she'd leave the house to me but she knew I loved it far more than she did ------ wasn't she always condemnin' it and sayin' all the things that annoyed her about it ? "It's far too big. Them stairs would kill you. That parlour would founder you. That passage would clean corn. There's far too much garden, sure we don't need the half of it !"

Say now, for instance ------ if the Missus dies and leaves me the house, I'd have to keep on with the fishermen to pay the bills, let the land the way we always do and I'd be happy to do all that ----- but what if some of the childer came back and wanted a share ? Where would I be then ?

Do you think it would be wise to give yer man the come-on ? Wouldn't it be better to invest for the future ? I could be fairly stuck lookin' at that auld Jinny all day and I bet you he'd live to a hundred he's that careful of himself !! Oh my, my ------- Life's not easy and I'm only fifty, there's plenty of life in me yet.

I didn't sleep much last night, the Missus had an auld dose of the flu and she's not rightly over it yet, it tuk a lot out of her. I was just goin' over and over the pickle I've got myself into. I heard of a fella in Newcastle who's a dab hand readin' the cups, Joe somebody-or-other, I wonder if he could advise a superior woman like m'self ------ Not that I have any grand ideas about m'self but I would have prospects, you know.

There's a wee woman above there in Rostrevor, Minnie the Caddy they call her and it's the cups she reads too or maybe it's the palms ------- I think I'd trust that man better. Oh aye ----- there's a fortune teller about Forkhill that a lot of the young ones go to, Mick was tellin' me one day ---- Och, I dunno !! Mick has the local hackney cab and he would take you any place, but if I let Mick take me to Forkhill, maybe he'd think he was on to a good thing, for he's on his own now too. Nice and all as he is I couldn't stomach him either. If I got him to drive me to Newcastle he'd spoil whatever chance I had with this Joe fella, for I hear he's a fine-lookin' man with his own house and a bit of land. Maybe he could be doin' with a good sensible woman to cook and clean for him and you wouldn't know what could come out of that.

And what about the fisherman ? Sure I'd have to go and live in Belfast, I've never been there before and I'd only get lost ! He's got a nice big car so maybe he'd want to come back here to fish, stay in Brown's hotel and I'd be all alone in Belfast ------ Naw, that's definitely him out !!

Where did I put that leaflet till I get the bus times for Newcastle ?

The Fortune Teller: Howareyizalldoin

M'names Joseph right enough, but sure I niver get nuthin' but Joe or even auld Joe ! Ach, doesn't bother me either way. I used to work in England for a while in the fifties, there was good money there on the roads in them days for there was damn all here. Da farmed a lock a fields and kept a few beasts but there wouldn't hev been enough to keep the other fella and me too, so our James went aff till Americay and that was that. Oh aye, he did write a few times to the mother when he got married but I suppose he was busy and he wasn't much of a hand with the pen. They lived away out in the wilds someplace, and I forget what they called her ----- somethin' daft like, Amber May Silkinsky or that ----- Aye, and he niver come back.

    Da died and Ma needed me back here, so I came home to rid the place up a bit and stay a wheen of weeks, and then, be jaypers didn't Ma up and die on me too ! I just stayed on here for I was takin' no hurt and sure I knew every stick and stone about the place. Just me and Shep, the auld dog. Then I got a part time job in the forestry. When there was a bit of a rush on and they needed more they tuk me on. I liked that for it was quiet away up there in the mountain.

    When I was a bit younger I wouldn't hev minded getting married, for it's handy te hev a woman about the house, it makes the place a wee bit more respectable like. Anyway, by the time I thought of it there was nuthin' of interest round here in this parish. Either too old or too young and they'd have the last penny aff you, sure a man couldn't be bothered with that carry on. The new parish priest tried to warn me that it can be lonely for a man getting on in years and I should do something about it when I still could ------ but sure he's one to be talking and he seems happy enough !! Ach be jaypers, it's quare times we're livin' in. Sure if I tuk a woman now and she tuk a scunner to me, she could get me whole damn house and the bit a land and I'd hev nobody to blame but m'self ----- and it self-inflicted !! Sure I'm better aff the way I am ------ nobody te annoy me !

    The mother was blessed with the second sight and I've a wee bit of it too, although to tell you the truth it can be a bit of a curse at times ! I mind one day I was cutting back whins in the top field and I saw auld Mrs. Cunningham who wasn't out of her bed for years, straight as a ramrod walkin' down the loanin, plain as day she was. Mind you, I did think it a bit funny at the time. The very next morning, Francie the postman told me she died through the night. I've niver heerd the Banshee or anything but there y'are now ----- Wasn't that a good one ?

    Another time, down at the crossroads one evening I toul wee Davy that he'd soon meet a girl and marry before six months and be jaypers that was right ----- for he toul me he had te !! After that people began to ask me to tell their fortunes and it sort a snowballed. I swear to God it just happened and I seemed to be telling them the right things.

Then they wanted me te take money for it but sure I couldn't do that, I'm a straight man ye know. Forby, maybe I'd be telling them lies and wee stories and they only fit what I'm telling them to suit themselves ------ sure it's only a bit of craic !!

They started callin' at the house when it got too cowl to be sittin' on the ditch at the crossroads. When the nights started to draw in, I'd light the fire in the front room and as sure as I made a drop of tay there'd be a rap at the door. Maybe it would be a couple of wee girls wantin' me to tell their fortunes, so that's how I started to read the cups. All they would want to know is if they were goin' te meet a good-lookin' man with money and when ------ nuthin' else in their bloody heads only men and money. Ach weemin !!

The one thing Ma had was plenty of cups, thank God ! For many's a night I wouldn't a had time te rinch them out !! No, I niver tuk no money for that would hev meant bad luck for me ! If they brought me a packet of tay I niver refused and thanked them, for I went through plenty of it.

Aye ------ tay and biskits. In them days it was loose tay ye got from the grocer, we had none of them new-fangled tay-bags. They say it was only the sweepings of the flure that went into them tay-bags, sure it's like dust. Ye can't give it a good stew, no flavour at all, ye might as well just drink bog water !

The happiest days of m'life was them cowl winter nights or long summer evenings when there'd be a line of cars fornenst the house, vans and bikes up the loanin and young ones laughin' in the front room. People tuk their turn to come in, two or three at a time. Sometimes there be an auld one who fancied me, so I'd have to spin a good yarn there !! ------ Aww now boy, ye hav te watch yerself and there's no flies on Joe !!

    Sure, what was it but a drop of tay and me imaginin' wee pictures left in the tay leaves at the bottom of their empty cups, if it made them happy sure it made me happy ! The mother would have been happy too, for nobody was ever turned away from this house without a cup in their hand ------ Aye, she would have had me sweepin' and dustin' if she thought there was strangers in her front room. That's weemin for ye. Sure, a bit of dust niver did no harm ------- aren't we all made of it and back to it we'll go.

    I'm away on now, God bless and good luk te ye. That sky's changing ------ we'll have rain before the day's out.

No Kidding

Shouldn't admit this of course. I don't like wee new babies much, never have, never will. I just can't "Oooh" and "Aaaw" over them the way most people can !

Now, when they evolve into proper little persons, well that's a completely different matter. I love them, they are terrific. I remember taking a first sideways look at this tiny scrap of humanity, who had so nearly cost me my life and saying out loud to him "Well Buster, you better be strong and make the best of things because I don't think I'm cut out for this motherhood lark ----- I promise I'll try but please don't be too disappointed."

Anyhow, thanks to a husband who loved tiny, fragile babies and things, a very supportive mother and mother-in-law, sisters and sister-in-law ------ you were fed, watered, washed and changed in quick succession all day, every day, never noticing, I hope, my complete lack of interest. I think there's a medical term for it nowadays.

After a few months, four or five maybe, you began to take a look at things. Smile, make noise, cry, hiccup, cry, smile. Cry when hungry. Cry when sleepy. Cry when wet and uncomfortable. Cry when colicky. You were becoming real to me and I began to lose the fear and mistrust I had of you. We had great chats, you and I.

Two years and two months later, shock number two

arrived. WOW ! How in Heavens did this happen ? Smirk, if you must but they didn't tell us a lot about contraception in those days ! Everyone assumed everyone knew all these things but truth to tell ----- we all knew very little and just bluffed our way through !

Number two was a girl who always knew what she wanted from the word go (and still does !) Again, the family took pity on this incompetent young mother. I found it difficult to do twice as much work, in half as much time. You see, work priorities and order were never my strong point. My reading, foutering about, wasting time and day-dreaming were getting neglected. Having to change not one set of nappies but two, making feeds, sterilizing bottles, plus endless washing, cooking and making lists, wasn't leaving much time for Irish poetry, Asian cookery or even a glimpse of yesterday's newspaper. At least you could talk to me, keep me in craic, even if I couldn't understand all your lingo and all the things you said about your wee sister. She was fast becoming an interesting, busy little person too.

All was going sort of well and BINGO ! Thirteen months later, number three arrived. Boy again, black haired, very tanned and laid back. You see the other two were quite blonde and fair skinned, but this one due to the exceptionally good weather and also that most of the pregnancy had been spent outside in the sun every day ! After a while, he too developed into a little person with his own ideas and thoughts about things. So there we were, a young couple, three kids, all with completely different personalities, all fighting for space in the debris of scattered toys, mountains of washing, spilt milk, plastic beakers, lost shoes, broken things, dirty cups, endless ironing, trying to keep the show on the road.

By now, I had a fair idea of what caused all this chaos and children. It just shows you all the same, don't believe everything people tell you, like "You won't get pregnant if you eat plenty of plums" or "Make love if there's a full moon" !

We had a great crop that year and boy, you should have seen the harvest moon. Yep, that was it. VOILA ! Number four arrived with hardly a ripple on the pond !! Somebody told him, I think before he was born, if you do as you're told, make good friends with a dog or other animal and don't make too much noise, you won't get into trouble ! All that is quite a while ago and for me the growing up years quite outshone the fearsome baby days.

Guess what ? Bet I'm the only reluctant mum who cried when told she was going to be a granny for the first time !! I've watched them grow up and now how privileged, proud and happy I feel when the good-looking grandsons and granddaughters come to visit, telling me of their hopes and dreams.

I wonder what the next generation will bring ?

Purple Herby's First Family

John and his boys in France

Hindsight is a ------ wonderful thing ! There I was, trying to pack the minimum for a first-time, continental camper van trip with the husband and four (no, FIVE !) children, catching a flight to Paris first to pick up the camper he had organised weeks earlier.

     WHY, WHY, WHY ------ wouldn't a weekend in a caravan at Cranfield have done just as well ? It seemed like a good idea at the time. A taste of France for the children without the long-haul drive down through Scotland, England and across the channel. Pick up the pre-booked Volkswagen camper van in Paris and stay the first night in a pre-booked four-star camp site there, what could go wrong ?

"If all goes well", he said, "We could dander down to Italy but don't get too excited", as back he went to pack all his own gear and all his maps. Don't forget this was in the days before mobile phones, sat-navs, electronic gadgets and broadband !

A friend who had done all this kind of thing before, told me to put everyone's wet weather gear in a big clear plastic bag, all the swimwear with the sun hats in another and one warm sweater for each of the children in another, "Saves a lot of hassle" she said !

The children all had their own small rucksacks each for their needs. Mine, bit bigger of course, had the first aid kit, cough mixture, the TCP, the mosquito salve, tomato ketchup for those who couldn't live without it, Irish tea bags, scissors and Sellotape, sunburn lotion, all the sore tummy and essential stuff. "Mum, do we have ------ ?" "No, we haven't got any and you don't need it here !!" Apart from my old jeans, a couple of tee-shirts and a pair of shorts, some underwear, that was it.

The husband's rucksack had maps galore, screwdrivers in various sizes, pliers, small pieces of rope, small torches, two pairs of shorts, two pairs of sunglasses, assorted tee-shirts, several pairs of socks, enough clean underwear for two weeks and dear knows what else ------ oh and a small bottle of whiskey for emergencies ! His big folder had all our passports and travel documents, I must say he's very good at that !

The next morning, Grandfather kindly drove us to Dublin airport to catch the Paris flight. Had us there in good time, said our goodbyes, listened to Grandfather's endless advice, did a head count, all present and correct, checked in and made our way to the aircraft with the other travellers, when directed.

I had supervised the children packing (honestly !) but I had not spotted number two son with a battered old tin teapot tied to the outside of his small rucksack until he was clanking his way down the aisle of the plane and I was the one getting amused looks from the already seated passengers ! Where on earth did he find that ? I could see folk saying to each other. God help that woman with the squad of youngsters, must be a school outing with their teachers. How wrong could they be ? I tried to look happy and smiled as I walked after the teapot man. "They're not all ours !" I wanted to shout at them (the passengers, I mean).

The husband had gone ahead to help get the rucksacks into the overhead lockers and find their seats. We had our three boys but felt we should bring our only daughter's wee friend, company for her and, so far, all was working out well. The idea was that the girls would help me with the camping chores and the boys would help their dad, on this our first, family continental holiday, an educational trip, one they would always remember !

Arriving at Paris airport was a bit overwhelming for our youngest, who wanted to go home "RIGHT NOW

PLEEEESE !" However, after going through customs, having to open his rucksack like everyone else and with promises of the camper van waiting for us, he soon settled down. After lugging our two trolley loads of baggage, a quick bite to eat for everyone from the first fast food outlet we saw, roll call again, all present and correct, we made our way to the area where the camper was supposed to be. Wrong area, try again, more walking. "Need the toilet, Mum !" Me ----- "Thought you'd all been there in the main airport, there's none here, can't you wait a few minutes ?" Dad ----- "We can go back, we've just passed some." The convoy stopped, backtracked and those who had to go went. Two seconds later, two disgusted and astonished faces appeared. "Mum, they are smelly, it's AWFUL ! When you flush the water gushes over your feet !!!" (Don't forget this was France in the Seventies !) More walking, endless parked vehicles, wrong area, try again. Look, third down the line is a PURPLE VW camper van, yes, yes it seems right this time ! Dad consulted his papers, opened the driver's door, looked in, checked his papers yet again and decided it was ours. The excitement was indescribable !! We stowed the luggage, left the trollies back to a trolley dock and all piled in. We're here at last !

"Mum, Mum, Mum - Look at this !! Look ! Dad, Dad, Dad - look, look !" ("Oh Lord ! Where did I put those headache pills ? Oh, for a cup of tea !") My husband had the directions to Camp Beauville well studied, so off we headed into the unknown. Yes, he had driven in France and Canada a few times before with friends but this was different, with the wife and a van load of kids ! "My goodness, it's only six o'clock here, nearly dusk and still so warm, will it be even hotter tomorrow ?"

Arrived at the camp, just before dark, checked in and found our parking site. The kids had a quick run around the area, while I opened the cool box and set out the night time bikkies and cool drinks. After a short time sorting out the sleeping arrangements, finding the supplied sleeping bags, a last trip to the loo, hands and faces washed, safely zipped into their sleeping bags, the long day's travel and excitement took its toll and ten seconds later, not a squeak from any of them !

Himself and I, had a quiet nightcap, breathed a sigh of relief, thanked God and called it a day too, segregated in our own private quarters. "So far, so good. Tomorrow's a new day and just imagine ------ there's going to be TWO whole weeks of this excitement !!"

Morning dawned bright, clear and hot. We glanced in behind the curtain at the happy campers in their disarray. Sleeping bags in a heap on the floor, five rosy pink faces, ten bare legs and ten bare arms stretched out at all angles and not an open eye between the lot of them ------- Bliss for another while !

Purple Herby: A Mind of its Own

When the Volkswagen factory had finished with me, I was a handsome fellow. They had painted me in their latest colour, at least they said it was their latest colour, sort of purply. I would have preferred that limey green they did. Purple is an old person's colour I think. Anyway, I had no say in the matter so purple it was !

They did a good job on my innards too. Plenty of fitted cupboards for the cups, plates, cutlery and things on the wall above the plastic sink unit, next to it was a mini fridge with a cupboard underneath, all covered by a big-hinged lid which made a great worktop for dumping things on ! There's a double gas mini-oven for cooking and a drop leaf table. Two neat wardrobes for coats, bedding and extras and the bench seats in the cabin turn into comfortable beds at night, with more storage underneath. Oh yes, they had thought of everything !

They had given me one of these big sunshine roofs, the whole thing pushed up to give standing up room in the cabin. Thank goodness it wasn't that awful concertina type, that pushed up to one side only and caused panic when people caught their fingers in the mechanism ! They didn't skimp on the chrome either and the VW badge on my nose was a decent size, an improvement on the earlier model I thought. Earlier models had a spare wheel perched on their nose and that made people think the wheels were not reliable. All in all, I was quite happy with my appearance.

The one thing about VW's, their engines are good, so you didn't have to worry about that. You had to watch some of these holiday drivers though, once they got behind the wheel they enjoyed driving so much they forgot all about tyre pressure, checking oil and water, simple maintenance. That was a laugh, I can tell you. I used to scare the Divil out of them if I thought they were careless. (It's a secret how I did it ---- clue, it's to do with the brakes !)

Did I tell you that I was a rental vehicle ? I would dearly have loved to belong to a family with children or a young couple and have adventures with them, if they could afford me ! I was quite expensive when I was new, you know. The firm who bought me was one of these multi-rental companies, in fact they owned four of us VW's. They kept replacing us with new models every two or three years and then we were sold, (well maintained, secondhand !) unless some of the holiday clients had crashed us and we were a write off, you wouldn't believe how stupid or careless some folks can be !

Anyway, there I was, sitting in this posh garage showroom in Paris on my first day, all clean and sparkling, feeling a bit nervous and homesick for the VW's noisy, smelly workshop, wondering who on earth would be my first guests. Next morning, Monsieur Boss-man, I can't remember his name, came out of his office waving a bit of paper and shouting at another guy to get that new rental out to the airport immediately, there's an Irish family checking in this afternoon, (all this was in French, you know !) I didn't think for one minute it was me he was referring to. There were a few other new campers of different makes in the showroom and on the forecourt, so flip me, I couldn't believe it when the guy jumped into my driver's seat, backed me out of the showroom and took off like a racing driver, down a maze of side streets ! Talk about fright, I'd never been driven on any street before. I'd been brought to the showroom straight from the factory, on top of one of those big transport carriers with several others ! My tyres had NEVER EVER touched the dust of any road and here I was, zooming down narrow Paris streets and me with no control at all over where we were going ! Oh, mon Dieu ! (as they say in France), We are all going to be kilt ! (as they say in Ireland)

Anyway, Pierre or whatever his name was, certainly knew his way around Paris. He whizzed me through busy junctions with four or five lanes of traffic and, before I caught my breath, had parked me in a special bay at Charles de Gaulle Airport, took his slip of paper, locked me up and disappeared with my key.

I sat for a while and tried to relax, pretending to a grubby-looking Renault camper van parked next to me, that this was all in a day's work. He kept looking down his nose and glancing at me sideways but I could see he was having a sneaky Gauloise fag, in spite of all the big "No Smoking" signs. I ignored him, closed my eyes and waited. After some time, a trendy-looking couple, the guy clutching a sheaf of papers, arrived at the Renault. He began walking around it, consulting his papers and giving off a bucketful in an excited torrent of French or something, to his lady friend who completely ignored him. She carefully set down her small case, took a mirror from her handbag and began to adjust her hair and make-up. He was not a happy bunny !

I was hoping they were not my clients and I was scared to look sideways at them. After a lot of pacing around the Renault, much waving of papers and, I guess, bad language, he stomped off with his lady love trailing behind him. Bad choice if he was trying to impress her. I don't think a weekend in a beaten up camper van was her kind of treat, more like a five-star hotel with all the trimmings, if they'd asked me !!

I took a sideways look at my neighbour but he appeared to be resting and had his eyes closed. Presently, I heard running feet and loud chatter, Sounds like a herd of children, I thought. Good grief, I hope they are not coming this way ! More footsteps, a man and woman appeared. He had a small child by one hand, a sheaf of papers and my key in the other, she had a loaded trolley of luggage, which some older children were helping her push and a small boy was doing wheelies with the other loaded trolley. Daddy-man had stopped beside me and consulted his papers for a minute or two. When he seemed satisfied he opened up the cab and got in. After a quick inspection, he jumped out and said with a smile, "Well kids, this looks like the start of our adventure, what do you think ?" Then Daddy-o pulled back the sliding door, halfway up my left hand side, Mum got in first, gave a very happy laugh and we (the kids and I), knew I'd passed the test !

After the bags were stowed in the back and the children had chosen their seats, (no separate child seats back then !) Mum got in the front passenger seat beside Daddy-o, she always did navigator and kept Daddy-o right on family trips. They had the first camp site chosen and booked earlier, Daddy-o had the route well-rehearsed. I could see that he had driven on the wrong side of the road (to them) before and seemed very confident ------ so I wasn't all that worried. It was nearly dark before we saw the big camp site all lit up, drove in and found the office. Daddy-o checked in and was given our designated parking place number. We had a lovely big space under some chestnut trees, not too close to our neighbours, who had a different make of camper van and two small tents set up but there was nobody in sight.

The whole family jumped out, had a quick survey of the place before Daddy-o rounded them up to do their camping chores. Ho ho ! I thought. This lot have been out before ! They visited the toilet and shower block, found where the fresh water taps were, the boulangerie where the fresh croissants, baguettes and petit pain would be sold for breakfast and, most importantly, where the children's play park was ! I just sat there quietly, letting my engine cool down and watched. I was surprised how quickly five pairs of short legs could cover the main area, find all the necessary places and report back to the parents ---- Yes, this lot had definitely been out before !

I had no experience of this camping lark ----- only what the other VW's who had experience told me, when they came back into the factory for refurbishment and service. Of course, some of the stories they told were intended to scare the wits out of a beautiful, brand new camper like me ! Surely they couldn't all be like that ---- could they ?

I was glad my lot seemed to know what they were about, though time will tell ! They all piled in, Daddy-o set up the table, Mum opened the big cool bag and produced a ready-made supper in no time at all ! I was worrying about their sleeping arrangements. Mum had them organised, found the new sleeping bags in the wardrobe and let each choose their own. Daddy-o turned the rows of seats into beds, curtained off the parent's quarters and all were fast asleep in no time ! It had been a long day for them --------- me too ! I'm beginning to like them I think, but they never stop asking questions !

The next morning it was bright and sunny, trees, birdsong, banks of perfumed mimosa just outside, sandy paths leading to where ? Just then, three children walked past us and I could see they had been swimming, must be a pool somewhere ! So early !

My lot are still fast asleep, all of them ! Even Mum and Dad are having a lie in. Please don't ask me to drive anywhere just yet ! I do like the way they have pulled the curtains around all the windows and my windscreen and left the roof a little open for fresh air. It's so cosy in here, just another half hour please ? Then I'll be ready for anything !

Purple Herby: On the Road Again

Hello there, me again, Purple Herby. How have you been since last I saw you ? I'm still based in Paris. Me ? I'm fine now thanks.

Think I told you about my travels with the Irish family and all their kids, it sure was a busy trip but I learned a lot about this camping lark ! After we returned to Paris and they left me with many tears and promises to come back next year, I was sent to the VW depot to be cleaned and serviced. This Irish family certainly clocked up the miles, we ended up in Yugoslavia, now known as Croatia, by way of Italy and the weather was very, very hot. Anyway, after the service and tidy up (actually, the family were very good, no major breakages or scrapes, Daddy-o had taken great care of me !) I was sent back to the airport to await my next client.

Well, it turned out I had to wait quite a few decades for another memorable vacation but I am an extremely patient van, just like any other self-aware vehicle has to be !

So, one day I was just waiting as usual in the airport, when this good-looking big lad appeared with a very large rucksack, a bandana round his long hair, guitar and papers in his hand, I expected the rest of his party would follow. Wrong again ! He briefly checked his papers, threw his pack in the back, jumped into the driver's seat and consulted an armful of maps. He didn't even have a look to see how the cooking facilities or the water tank worked. I really wanted to tell him how comfortable the beds were and how simple the roof was to raise. Well, we must have sat for about an hour while he worked his way through umpteen maps and leaflets with a felt tip pen. I naturally thought he was waiting for somebody arriving from a later plane and had just closed my eyes for forty winks when he suddenly flashed into action. He checked the lights and brakes and that all my door locks were working, petrol tank was full and the tyres were in order ------ Not so stupid for a young fella, eh ? I thought, but why no company ?

Anyway, we took off into town in brilliant sunshine at maximum speed, with my windows down and the radio blaring. We shot past a row of old timers and gave them a blast or two of the horn, just to get the feel of things -------- Wow, this is going to be a lot different from the last family !! After an hour and a bit, we were well out of the city and heading north, the traffic was getting lighter. I just wish he would take me into his confidence as to what his itinerary is, where's our destination, etc. I had no bother with the Irish family as they were always yakking ----- talking, asking questions as to where we were going and how long would it take to get there ! Eventually, we stopped at a fast food complex and he stocked up on bottled water and not a lot more. Interesting, huh ? Last week it was food, food and more food !

On we went, for at least another hour until we came to an isolated camp site out in the sticks. Oh, it was clean OK but basic ----- not like the camp sites I had stayed in with the Irish family, all four-star jobs. I suppose it was a bit early in the evening. I did smell a barbeque starting up somewhere close by and I could hear music. My young man went off to check in and eventually came back with a pack of beer and something to eat from the site carry out. I was disappointed he didn't even try to cook on my gleaming stove. He took a rug out of the wardrobe, set it on the grass, sat down, opened a can of beer and started on his curry. I hadn't noticed that he had one of these funny, mini click-click, computer things and a big file beside him too ---- Good Lord ! This new technology is something else ! (Don't forget we are going back some years !) The warm evening passed slowly with him still sitting on the grass, consulting his file, tapping on this computer thing now and then and drinking more beer. I was utterly bored stiff ------ no craic at all here.

Just when I thought it was time for all serious campers to pack up for the night, two camper vans rolled in and parked across the way from us. They seemed to be old VW vans all done up and plastered with some sort of graffiti. In no time at all, they had a barbeque set up, with fancy lights over the top and around their wagons, it all looked so cheerful. Our man just gathered up his gear, went inside, set up all his files, books and stuff on the table, turned on the light and carried on working as he had before the newcomers arrived.

Time passed, I could see that our neighbours seemed to be two couples and they seemed to be sharing their meal together, it sure smelled yummy, whatever it was ! The evening wore on and our guy was still at his books, I was just resting and bored stiff. Suddenly, I could hear a guitar strumming from over there, it sounded good. After a while, Jake (I nicknamed him Jake --- I think it sounds pretty cool) stood up, stretched, looked over at the newcomers, took his guitar from its case, stepped outside the door and ambled over to speak with the neighbours.

The other two couples said they were planning to travel to Denmark, spending a month and taking in some of the big music gigs. Jake told them he was studying for his finals and thought a bit of peace and quiet away from everyone was what he needed. They all seemed to gel with the music alright. Jake nipped back over to me, brought over the rest of his beer and one of his packets of crisps ! The moon appeared all big and shiny, the music went on and on, then another couple appeared from out of the bushes ! They'd been drawn by the music too. You know, I was so happy to be part of this younger group, it was what I'd hoped for when I was just qualified. I had wanted to be owned by a family with children or a young couple and have adventures with them. Last week, I had the family bit and now who knows what excitement's in store for me now !

Next morning we set off quite early, after Jake had bought a coffee and a croissant for himself from the amenity block near the office. I should have said he had already had a short walk and spent at least an hour at his books, I don't understand him at all. You'd think if he was on holiday, he would want to see more of the area and the pretty villages near the camp site. He didn't even say au revoir to the folk across the way but sure there was no sign of anyone and the windows of their wagons were all closed up ----- OK Jake, on you go sunshine, full steam ahead to where ? Surprise me !

The afternoon found us at a lovely secluded beach, no official camp site but lots of big sand hills, off the main road, miles down a side road and miles along a deserted track. Talk about solitude. Out came the blanket, the beer and the books, all set up in a sandy corner, out of the sea breeze. Way over to the right was an outcrop of rocks, I don't know if Jake would have noticed it, but I did. The tide was coming in and splashing over the base of the rocks. Sun ----- sea ----- solitude, I closed my eyes ----- bliss !

Something woke me, I looked again and I was nearly sure, or was it my imagination ? I thought I saw a pretty girl sitting on the rocks, with long blonde hair, she had her back to us. I looked over at Jake but he was still immersed in his books. I wanted to shout at him but suddenly felt like I didn't want to share the moment. The girl on the rocks turned and looked back at me, smiled and immediately I felt we were friends. Just then, she floated into the water and with ease became part of it. She just disappeared while I watched.

Jake was still concentrating on his work but after a minute or two he got up and stretched his legs. He walked over to the edge of the sea, picked up a few pebbles and skimmed them out to sea. It's uncanny but honestly, I saw a blonde head appear just beyond the rocks. The blonde hair seemed to float in the water but the movement under the water seemed to be heading back to the rocks. In a moment or two, the girl was perched back on the rocks and I could see a long fish tail ----- Good grief ! Was this girl a mermaid ? Och, would you wise up Herby, things like that just don't happen !!

By this time, Jake was still picking up pebbles and skimming them out to sea, he was pretty good at it. Then the figure on the rocks caught his eye, he did a double take and believe it or not, he just picked up more pebbles and fired them into the sea as before ------ the stupid big ! I was afraid of him scaring off the mermaid girl, she looked so pretty and fragile but boy, could she swim !

I really thought this was no place for me, curious and all that I was, so I just closed my eyes. Wise move. Two hours later I woke up, lo and behold you, there was Jake sitting on the rock beside Mermaid Milly ! Two hours later, Milly (now without her tail, wearing jeans and tee-shirt !) was sitting on the rug beside Jake, right under my engine and my nose. Looking into each other's eyes and chatting away like they had known each other all their lives. The books, files and precious guitar were scattered on the ground beside them ! Not my business anyway.

I often wonder, did he get his degree ?

Fisherman's Friend

Isn't it funny how a chance remark to someone can change your whole life ? That's what happened to me some years ago. One day when I was shopping in Newry I accidentally met a man I had known years previous at college.

Of course, the conversation was all about catching up on life, marriage and children. I was giving him the low down on our four who were of a similar age to his three. I can remember that at that time our seventeen-year-old eldest son was giving us problems. He was car mad and was having driving lessons but had not yet passed his test. One evening as my husband and I were returning home we met our son on the road driving my car accompanied by some of his mates and related this horror story to my friend, saying I didn't know what we'd do with him when the school holidays started.

About a week later my friend phoned to ask if we thought our son would be interested in a summer job in Germany as his firm in the Kilkeel fishing industry had connections with fishing factories on the coast near Hamburg, accommodation would be provided and he could bring a friend. We (and he) thought this was a wonderful opportunity, Paul knew that it was a starting-at-the-bottom job shovelling herring. Anything to get away from the parents for the Summer and get paid too !

We discussed it with his friend's parents and they readily agreed. We left the boys to Dublin airport for the Hamburg flight in great excitement, with promises from them of good behaviour and frequent phone calls home (no mobile phones then !)

The fishing town was called Cuxhaven, Hamburg was the nearest airport so the boys had to get themselves there by train. After a few days the first phone call came, all was going well, food was yuk but they were getting to like it and they could curse fluently in four languages ! We were hoping they would learn to speak German properly, we hadn't thought about eastern European countries !

The boys loved their time there that first Summer and couldn't wait to get back the following year and the following and the following. Cuxhaven turned out to be a great place for overseas students and many of the fish factories depended on them for summer jobs. Some years later my husband and I took our camper van to Germany and visited Cuxhaven which looked to me like Kilkeel harbour but at least twenty times as big !

Needless to say, many friendships, romances and marriages were made and that's how we have a wonderful extended German family with our son who still lives there and our grandchildren.

So many happy memories of holidays there with them and the pleasure of having them home here to Rostrevor.

Hello Sailor !

Coming from a family with friends, young and old, who enjoyed and loved sailing, especially the racing on Saturday afternoons, the vibes somehow missed me out.

    Oh yes, I had no problem making the sandwiches, packing the bottles of juice and perhaps something stronger if needed, finding the misplaced sailing gear, warm socks and such necessities for those going on a day's sailing in wee boats. I'd have the evening meal ready in a flash, for the crew ------- when I could actually see the boat coming in to the mooring near home, as time doesn't come into sailing. "Should be back around six" could mean anchoring about eight or nine depending on weather and then there's all that tidying up to do ! For me, I could enjoy the replay of what happened out on the lough, the "We could have made better time if the wind hadn't suddenly dropped just then", to the "We should have gone about sooner !" ----- Gone about where ? I often wondered.

    Then there were moves to bigger boats, with bigger sails, bigger engines, living space called a "cabin", kitchen called a "galley", toilet and shower downstairs ----- sorry "below" called the "heads". Still, it was very nice and comfortable to sit out on the deck in the sunshine, if there was any. Drink a hot coffee or a glass of wine and let those who knew what they were doing get on with the leppin' about: changing sails, giving orders to each other and shouting "Lee Ho" every now and then. Very hard remembering all the funny names though, even your husband, son-in-law or friend, if they were the owner or in charge of the boat were called "skipper", reminded me of a tin of sardines !

Ahh well, I'm not complaining because I have many happy and funny memories, and a few doubtful ones too, of my sailing days. My husband's boat at that time was a smart, little white painted job with a blue band around the top, two nice white sails, one with blue numbers on it (I do like things to be colour coordinated) and I think there was a small extra one called a "spinnaker". There were two bunk beds in the pointy end called a "bow", a folding table beside the wall, sofa in the cabin, a sink unit and a little primus for making the tea. Bit cramped I thought, but apparently it was the speed the boat could travel under sail that counted, not passenger comfort !

Oh yes, there was an outboard engine that hung over the back of the boat in case of an emergency. For me, the main problem was getting on to and off it. Our boat was called "Footloose", moored in the sea in front of our house, which meant getting into one of those inflatable dinghy things and being rowed out to it. Well, getting into the dinghy at the edge of the water while carrying the bag of goodies is one thing, but getting out of it is another story ! Climbing up on to the deck of another boat from an inflatable dinghy alongside, calls for a lot of courage and balance. Standing up with the dinghy bobbing up and down in the water, feeling strung up, with the life jacket on over the big sailing jacket. Trying to look cool and gripping the skipper's helping hands for a big heave up on to the deck with my wee short legs, believe me, is not easy !

Once aboard and settled comfortably, watching the changing scenery, waving at passing craft and keeping an eye on the choppy waves, the fear subsides a bit. That is until the skipper suddenly pulls on a rope connected to the sails, shouts Lee Ho or something and then everyone jumps to the seats on the opposite side of the boat, which makes it keel over to one side, nearly touching the water and then take off like a bat out of Hell ! By now, you understand I am slightly out of my comfort zone but determined not to let my discomfort spoil others enjoyment. Ahh well, I'm good at passing round the sandwiches and buns when the time comes. Meanwhile, I sit tight and don't get in the way of those who do the leppin' about adjusting things.

Years later, when Ken, a friend who lived in Scotland acquired a beautiful yacht, he kindly asked my husband and I with another couple of friends, to join him on a cruise through some of the Scottish lochs. I was really looking forward to this trip as I had heard that the new boat was equipped with every degree of comfort and navigational equipment imaginable, not that I doubted Ken's sailing prowess !

I knew we would be away for at least a week and that posed the old question every woman contends with when facing an unknown situation; what on earth clothes should I bring ? Warm jackets and warm trousers if it's cold, lighter things if it turns out to be a scorching week ----- a bikini ? The obligatory wet weather gear, maybe there'd be a visit to a posh restaurant beside a marina we could be moored at and all that had to be packed into as small a bag as possible ! At least I knew that high heels were definitely out, as was anything tight, revealing or skimpy ! For ladies in that position, old battered trainers or deck shoes, faded jeans and a sailing jacket that looked as if they had seen many a sailing trip (preferably with well-known top of the range labels !) is more acceptable and gives the impression to others that you've been sailing far and wide for years. In company, you can throw a couple of one-liners about "jibs", "cringles" or "halyards" and they are none the wiser. Oh, don't forget to leave the lipstick and eyeliner at home, along with the hair rollers ! The classiest lady crew all sport the au natural look.

    Walking through the busy marina to our friend's yacht with all our gear in the trolley was so exciting. Hundreds of yachts and motor cruisers were moored, some quite modest, some large, some very large and some were the "Oh, look at me, aren't I just gorgeous" kind !

    My friend and I tagged along behind Ken and our husbands, wondering which of these beautiful craft was going to be home to us for the next week and keeping an eye on what other sailing wives or girlfriends aboard their boats were wearing. Stepping over the side of the yacht from the walkway called a "pontoon", was so much more dignified than trying to get aboard from a dinghy bouncing about in choppy water. My goodness, I had never seen such luxury on a boat before ! Wow, this is going to be a trip to remember. Big wide deck area, large spray hood covering a multitude of navigational necessities, the stair well for going below and providing shelter from the wind for those sitting on the deck.

Elizabeth and I were allocated the forward cabin (the pointy end of the boat !) Twin bunks, plenty of storage space, a proper loo and shower was just next door ------ IMAGINE !! There was another big cabin at the other end of the boat, behind the "saloon" which had a big table flanked on three sides by comfortable bench seating, galley with a large cooker, fridge freezer, a sink unit and proper steps for going upstairs !

Our skipper was a wonderful cook, the hospitality was five-star, the husbands helped with the sailing chores and we helped where we could. Wow, this was the life ! Next morning as we set off, I did wonder how Ken was going to get us safely out of our berth in the middle of all those other expensive-looking craft, without bumping any of them but it was no trouble to him and soon we were out in the loch with the wind behind us, sails up, zooming our way to the next port of call.

Every day was a new experience for us and the short visits we made to many of the little villages was so interesting. One day, from our position on the water, we could see several American flags fluttering in the distance through the trees around a small village. Skipper Ken, with our approval thought it would be worth investigating. He duly dropped the sails and motored us into their small harbour, tied us up beside the wall, which had steep rusty iron ladders in places along it. Lovely little harbour to look at, but my heart sank when I realised we were going to have to climb up this high ladder if we were going to see what was going on up there with all the flags and music. I would have been quite happy to stay aboard and wait for the others to come back but they were having none of it. I managed to get my foot on the first rung of the ladder and with one of the crew in front of me and another behind me, I gripped the hand rails tightly, closed my eyes and climbed up the twenty or so rungs by feel, sprawling out on to the tarmac on all fours when I got to the top ! Oh, the indignity of it, it was awful !

The first thing we saw was a bearded man in a black suit wearing a black bowler hat, leading a donkey and carrying a very large bible under his arm ! He told us it was Country and Western Week and everyone dressed up in old-American style. We saw several John Wayne and Magnificent Seven types, many Annie Get Your Gun types and several "floozies" outside the many bars and shops which were all decorated in the American Wild West style. We were told that this was an annual event on the island, C&W groups and bands take over the place but if you live here and don't like loud music day and night, the best thing is to take a holiday. It was fun to see it happening for a couple of hours but I don't think I'd like a week of it ! So with one man in front of me and one behind me, my eyes closed, I reversed down that wee narrow ladder back to the safety of the boat !

We ate out on deck a lot and the seagulls were grateful for any scraps left over. Ken is an excellent cook, fond of hot chillies or curry in his dishes. One poor seagull was quite greedy and grabbed a bit of bread that had hot red chilli sauce on it, you should have heard him squawk as he dived to scoop up beakfuls of water. Bet he probably stuck to something he knew, like fish, after that experience !

Later on, in that glorious week we were heading up into Loch Long, going fast enough and doing enough knots to satisfy our skipper. After a time on the deck in the sunshine, liquid refreshment and all that, the thought occurred that maybe I should pay a visit below. Anyway, when I looked into our sleeping quarters, which we had left in a mess with discarded clothes, books, etc. I thought I should tidy up a bit.

This took longer than I expected, so by the time I had moved into the loo department I remembered that, at first a valve at the side of the toilet bowl had to be opened, to let the water come into the cistern to flush. I had just done that when the boat shuddered and started to behave something like a bucking bronco in a Western movie. The water started to slosh out in great quantities from the toilet bowl, all over my feet and the floor, gallons of it !! I thought we were surely going to sink !

This seemed to go on and on and on, me with my elbow jammed into the wash hand basin to hold steady, trying to stay upright and praying fervently that God would not let me drown and go down with the ship. By now I was soaked and never so scared in my life !! The boat seemed to quiver a bit and the awful bouncing seemed to slow down. I was soaked to the skin and the floor was under water but I was able to get into our cabin next door, strip off my wet clothes and find dry ones. Just then I heard stifled laughter from the deck, "You OK down there ?" called husband. "I effin' well am not !", I whimpered up to them with tears tripping me.

Apparently, we had strayed too close to the big nuclear base there and were soon apprehended by a search party in a fast military launch boat. They gave our skipper a stern warning and then took off at full speed, leaving us bouncing about in their strong wake. Perhaps they mistook us for Russian spies ? That was the one and only sailing experience that I would not want to repeat. Back on deck with my friends, I lapped up their sympathy, knowing full well that my predicament had made their day !

I've picked up a few sailing tips since then, so if I get a chance to crew again in a luxury yacht in good weather, count me in ! Any offers ?

A Load of Bull

Most people can remember the date of an exceptional day in their lives. I can't. Other than it was a glorious Sunday in very early Spring about eight years ago. A "pet day", as they say around here, no snow lying or slippery roads. Cold OK, but there was bright sun and a real hint of summer warmth to come.

After lunch my husband suggested we get geared up and go to see how his wee planting of trees were doing. He has a few acres of land about six or seven miles from where we live. A couple of good fields slope down to the road and over the stone wall at the top there's lots of whins and boulders, just past the "sheugh" the rough ground opens out, it's not exactly foot-of-the-mountain stuff but high enough to give wonderful views from Slieve Gullion to the Mournes. It's a lovely place to walk and away over to the left is the area where these young trees are planted. They are well fenced off to keep rabbits, deer or anything else that might feed on the young saplings out.

His plan sounded fine to me, so I donned the flat shoes and warm fleecy jacket, suggesting we bring a flask of tea and a few bikkies. Beautiful day, blue sky and all that, just the two of us and the dog. After a short drive we arrived at the gate to one of the fields. My husband got out, opened the gate, drove the car up into the field and parked at an angle. Remember these are steep wee fields, "hanging up" fields some might call them !

Before the dog and I got out, I asked him if he knew if Jim, the farmer who rented the land, had his cattle out yet (they would have been housed over the Winter). He said that he didn't know but he would walk up to the top first and have a look, as he knew I had a fear of anything big with four legs, or more !! Not that I'd be bad to them or anything, I just don't like them. I sat on in the car and promised Bounty the dog (in the boot) that soon she would be chasing rabbits. How that wee dog loved to chase anything that moved !

After a few minutes, I glanced in the mirror and saw the husband coming over the top of the hill at breakneck speed. No, he wasn't actually running but he was moving pretty quickly ! He opened the driver's door and asked "Where's the keys ?" ---- Before I could say "You have them", he banged the door shut and lept over the five barred gate, like an Olympic hurdler out on to the road.

It was then that I heard "thrump, thrump, thrump" and to my horror saw a herd of fifteen-thousand cattle stampeding towards the car !! Well, it was only about fifteen young bullocks, so I'm told. I was petrified and tried to get as low as I could on the seat, even trying to squeeze into the space for your feet, between the dashboard and the seat. Me !!! Not the tiniest person ! I covered my eyes and ears but I could feel the car rocking, with the big beasts on all sides nudging up against it. I opened one eye and nearly died when an enormously big bloodshot eye fringed with white hair was pressed up to the window staring at me !! Oh, my God !!! Bounty in the boot had the sense not to whimper. I know she was scared stiff too. Rabbits are one thing but what on earth are these ?

I could hear the husband shouting and thumping the iron gate with a stick to try and chase them away. I was too weak to see the funny side of it. I didn't appreciate him leaving me in my hour of need, even when he explained that there wasn't time to get the car out on to the road AND close the gate to keep the bullocks in. After all he said, they were curious and had only come over to say hello and see if we had any feed for them.

Huh ? I said, take me home and we'll picnic at the back door ----- it's safer ! Bullocks are fine as long as they're fillet steak with chips, onions and mushrooms !

The Chair

Right from she was a wee girl our daughter always loved chairs. She had a thing about them. When we visited the Grannies or the Aunties houses she always had HER chair.

Later on, when she was a student in Manchester, she used to buy the odd chair in dirty old junk shops and paint them wild colours. Just to cheer the place up a bit, she said. The grotty flats, I mean ---- not Manchester !!

A few years ago, an uncle died and very kindly left all the nieces and nephews a few pounds each, not enough to go mad with but enough to buy some wee thing that they fancied. Anyway, our one went to a local auction, spied an old armchair, put a small bid on it and lo and behold you, she got it. There weren't many at the auction that day and she was just lucky. As far as I remember, it was a warm sunny day and sure people would rather be out in the sunshine and not stuck in a dusty old auction room !

Our lassie was delighted with her bargain, landed it home here to us and plonked it at the window in our sun lounge. I hated it on sight ! It was far too big, took up too much space, was out of keeping with the other furniture, covered in a very cheap, garish fabric and badly needed a bit of TLC. Never mind, it will be away in a week or two, I thought. It was so heavy, and if you banged your shin on it you would be black and blue for a fortnight. Edwardian or not, I thought it was an eyesore. There it sat in all its tatty glory, in prime position (she was between jobs and flats) for longer than I had hoped. She just had no place yet for "Ted", as she called it. I threw a rug over it, added a matching cushion and you know, it didn't look so bad after all !

Funny thing though, everyone who came into the room made a beeline for this chair and got comfortable ! Now, the view from our window is lovely, I know. Not many people can look down on the beach a couple of yards away, watching the tide coming in until you could nearly touch it, the way we can. With the light and shadows on the Cooley Mountains, the sea changes colour and position every time you look. Oh yes, we know it's all there and it's wonderful but we glance at it and go and do something else !

Well I'm telling you, times have changed in our house. Now my greatest pleasure is to curl up in the big chair, with the binoculars and a cup of coffee, just watching all the shipping, marine birds and sea life going on within a stone's throw. I had never noticed all the wee sea birds, the oyster catchers, the guillemots, the sandpipers, the curlews, hoking in the seaweed for food after a storm, or took the time to identify the birds that pop in here to rest and feed after their long flights from faraway places. Now I let the ironing or the dishes wait, while I enjoy the greatest show happening right outside the window, thanks to the big chair. Oh yes, I did have him recovered and it was money well spent, now he's a real beauty !

When my daughter (now living in Scotland) phones, she always asks how Ted is. Sometimes I ask Ted who ? As we know a few Teds. Oh Mum, there's only one Ted in your house ! Every time she comes home she threatens to take Ted back to her home in Ayrshire. I know she's only kidding because she knows he's quite happy here, well loved, polished weekly and gives us all endless pleasure.

Retirement Years

Come Day, Go Day

No dear, Margaret, you wouldn't enjoy this book at all. You're far too young and anyway there's no sex or violence in it. Well, very, very little.

Margaret dear, can you hear me ? Wake up ! I think this will interest you, it's really for ladies who know how to make those multi-coloured net petticoats stiff again ----- do you remember the old sugar and boiling water dodge ? Of course you do ! Well, guess what ? They're coming back into style ! I saw one the other day in a charity shop and it looked absolutely gorgeous ! All pink lilac and purple and it just needed the sugar job done. The poor little dolly bird in the shop hadn't a clue of its value ----- 10p was all she wanted for it ! Why, I remember we would have paid at least nineteen and eleven, depending where you were shopping, and a lot more if it was in Robinson and Cleavers.

Remember how we used to wear them slightly below our drindle skirts ? ----- Off the shoulder blouse, flat ballet pumps and Heaven's above I saw a pair of them in another charity shop the other day too !! The big wide elastic belts with the four metal studs haven't appeared yet but give it time ----- Of course the wee blades in the shops wouldn't know how sexy a twenty-two inch waist clinched in a big belt below a pointy bra and two stiffy petticoats can look, not when they have a stud through their nose and a dirty big black tattoo on their neck. IMAGINE ! Disgusting !

Anyway, I think I'll go and ask her to hold it over for me until next week when I get my pension, I've spent this week's on the purple stilettos and matching clutch bag. I suppose I could have done without the silver cigarette holder, now that I'm not allowed to smoke ! I'll have a look around and see if I can find something nice for you too, Margaret dear.

Now I'll let you into a secret, this talk about style has made me think about all those dances and the good times we had. The Arcadia in Portrush, the Floral Hall, Queen's Hop on a Saturday night, Club Orchid, Caproni's ----- we did them all ! Oh, even The Plaza although we knew we shouldn't be there. Well ! I'm going to arrange for Elvis and Frank to come over and see us, maybe they'd bring Ella too if she wasn't too busy touring. Patsy Cline could sing "Crazy" for us like only she can. What about old Glen Miller and his "String of Pearls" and all that ? I'm sure he'd come dear, if you asked him. We'll say it's a special night for charity, after all, the shops can't do it all and charity begins at home !

I'm sure Matron and the staff would enjoy it, we could teach them how to boogie, jive, quickstep and foxtrot, we were experts ! Gosh, we could have a few smoochy slow waltzes for the oldies and they wouldn't need the zimmer frames ----- they could just hold on to each other ! ----- I'll just get on the phone right away after I have my nap now. Would you like me to ask the girl in the shop tomorrow if she could find another nice petticoat for you, dear ? I'm just so excited, I could ------ Zzzzzzzzzzzzzzz

Vacation vs. Holiday

Well, what's the difference anyway ? Both mean the same thing for most folk. Two weeks maximum for us, with different ideas for time out:

Warm sunny weather, brisk to strong breeze, smallish sailing boat, well equipped of course, comfortable berth in quiet harbour and a pint with like-minded sailing types in the evening (not for me !)

Warm sunny weather, foreign cities, museums, art galleries, good shopping, nice restaurants, hotels and theatre in the evenings (not for him !)

Warm sunny weather, large luxury cruise liner, too many people, organised pleasures and activities (not for us !)

We sussed it for the Autumn and, never having been to Nova Scotia before, booked a flight to Halifax the capital, an overnight stay in a hotel near the airport and one for the night before our flight home. We'll take a chance on the rest of our trip as it's not high season, there's bound to be lots of accommodation according to the tourist information ! No booking ahead, sure we don't know where we're going anyway !

Next morning, after a late breakfast, we picked up the pre-booked rental car with all the maps and a copy of "Doers and Dreamers" tourist information and we were off ------- to dear only knows where !

The first thing we noticed was the magnificent colour of the trees, we hadn't realised that it was the "Fall" with them. Second thing we noticed was how it was much warmer than we expected ! The third thing was how light the traffic flow was, on the out of town highways, with wonderful big wide highways practically all to ourselves ! After a map-reading consultation, we tossed a coin. Let's stick to the coast, take the provincial arterial Highway 103 and branch off to the Lighthouse Route.

So, Lighthouse Route here we come ! The navigator says this should take us around the coast, stopping off to investigate little seaside villages, with their wonderful fish restaurants (we hope) and harbours, with maybe a bit of whale watching thrown in ! We overshot the road to Peggy's Cove, which everyone in the hotel said we should visit but somehow, we had missed it. "Never mind, we'll catch it on the way back" we said. Chester was an interesting place for our first night, checked in to a flower bedecked inn. The owner was so pleased to have folk from Ireland staying, as it was her first day since taking over the ownership of this inn. We were guests of honour and treated accordingly ! Breakfast was a long leisurely affair before we went on our way, feeling we had made a lifelong friend.

Passed through beautiful areas and towns with German names, like Lunenburg, a UNESCO world heritage site and gave it a good look over. It's a magical town, perched on the edge of the Atlantic and on through to the Acadian region. The first of many reminders to each other, "We'll stay longer here next time we're back !"

The tourist guide magazine was right. We found something interesting around every corner, quaint inns and guest houses, many we stayed in were five-star heritage homes, where the friendly welcome and wonderful breakfasts made us want to stay more nights than our time would allow. Seaside villages and endless beaches to be explored, lobster suppers and scallops to be enjoyed. The names of many of the towns and villages reflect the homeland of the early settlers, like Liverpool, Clyde River, Westport, Clare and even Londonderry ! People are courteous and friendly, cars actually stop to let you cross the road without a pedestrian crossing, if you are out walking and want to ----- unbelievable for us !

Another thing that tickled us, the names they use for businesses i.e.

Bean There - coffee shop

Bean Here Before - coffee shop and deli (in another town)

Your Plaice or Mine - fish shop

The Udder Place - beautiful farmhouse bed and breakfast

Pane in the Glass - window and door repairs store

Soled Out - shoe shop and shoe repairs

Nobody's Inn - inn for sale

Curl Up and Dye - hairdressers

That's only a few, wish I could remember some more of them ! Oh yes, and a big blue truck with a sign THERE GOES JIM on the back of the cab ! That was quite a popular one, large trucks with the drivers name on it.

On up the coast, we were intrigued with the scenery. So many harbours and boat yards (to his delight) out in the countryside unexpected shopping centres with wonderful food supermarkets, like Sobeys and small individual farmer's markets selling fruit and their own produce, wonderful local craft stores (to my delight !) How I wished I could do my weekly shopping there ! Only a short time to investigate, buy something tasty for lunch, to picnic with along the way in some idyllic spot.

We were still following the Lighthouse Route on Highway 103, making many diversions. "I wonder what's down that road ? Let's go and see." We were never disappointed ! Always something to make us giggle. After making a very long detour, down a dirt (unpaved) road to where we thought the beach would be, we found ourselves outside a beautiful seaside mansion with a big notice on the gate saying "Beware ! Two dogs and two old farts live here". No, we didn't call, but maybe they would have made two visitors from Ireland very welcome !

Onward through the Kejimkujik National Park and

scenic drive, cutting off a large corner of the country as we wanted to see the fabled Annapolis Valley, the fruit and wine grape growing area.

Autumn, or the Fall as they call it, is a super time to visit, the spectacular colour of the trees and Summer had left a comfortable heat behind. Well, I can't speak for Winter, although I'm told its cold, very cold ! I do know that the fruit harvest is apples, plums and grapes for the wineries. The whole area had something to investigate that appealed to us both, be it the huge agricultural machinery for him the actual produce for me and the wine tasting for both of us !

Driving through the country, we were intrigued to see people and children in gardens or parks, seemingly talking together or gathered in large groups, here and there. Even though they all wore hats or had long hair, their heads all seemed to be the same size, then we discovered they were really PUMPKINS ! Stuffed and dressed with clothes, made to look like real people ! It was coming up to the big pumpkin festival time, all the wee villages and towns were trying to put on their best show. Some families would have pumpkin people sitting outside on their porch or perhaps mowing their lawn, competition was keen !

In no time at all, we were heading to the Bay of Fundy to see, if you time it right, the tidal bore. This is an extraordinary fifteen metre rise of the tide in a very short time, we wondered at the little boats hanging halfway up a cliff waiting for the tide to rescue them ! Then maybe time for another wonderful lobster supper with all the fixings, definitely not to be missed. Just so much to see in this area, from the Fundy Geological Museum, the Maritime Blues Festival, the Pumpkin Festival, to the national historic sites and so many more ------ and so little time to see it all. Straight down Highway 102 and back towards the airport and home. We'll be back, that's for sure ----- for sure ! This is only one small corner we've covered, so roll on next year ! Maybe then we'll take the Trans-Canada Highway through to Cape Breton, to see where it ends (or starts ?) The next parish from there, straight across the wide Atlantic, is Mayo.

That was the start of our love affair with the Maritimes, the first of many visits over the years.

Hide and Souk

The tour leader promised us an interesting two hours. She told us that the bus would be waiting for us at the south side entrance to the Souk "And be there on time, please !"

We started to file slowly out of the big comfortable air-conditioned bus, wondering if we should bring a cardi and perhaps a sun hat, or if we should leave the camera safely on board with the driver. Well, you never know in places like this, do you ? There's bound to be pickpockets. We were mostly middle-aged couples and a few ladies, of certain age reminding each other about things like sunglasses and purses, trying to edge the others in front to get a move on and get out. Several other tour busses had lined up too but their passengers were nowhere to be seen. There were not many white-robed locals to be seen either and it seemed a nice quiet street under the palm trees.

Our turn eventually and we could see why it took so long for some folk to get off the bus. A blast of searing heat made speaking almost impossible, hotter than opening the oven door washed over us. We stood a moment, while our eyes adjusted to the brilliant white light of the sun and tried to see where our guide had gone to. She waved her little green parasol, pointed to a small black entrance in the high white wall and our fellow travellers disappeared like mice down a hole into the Souk.

My sister and I stood for a moment, our money wallets well-tucked out of sight and with hands free made a dash for the entrance too. It was a little cooler inside there out of the burning rays of the sun. The other side of the wall was an unbelievable kaleidoscope of colour, heat, noise and masses of moving people. After drawing our breath to adjust to the melee, for there is no other word for it, we realised the din was the stall holders, men, women and children, all shouting their wares in an unintelligible language, each one louder than the other. The stalls were laid out like back alleys in no particular order and the smell of unknown vegetables and something rotten was overpowering.

After a few minutes, when we had been accosted by several enthusiastic vendors, we caught on that it was a good idea to walk purposely on and not to make eye contact. Even so, these big Arab guys in their long white shirts and shifty-looking youths in black were persistent. "Ladieeeee, Laideeeee, you buy my vegetables ? -------- So good for you ! I make you good price !" Always the same cry, "I make you good price ! ------ Lovely Laideeeees." "NO, NO ! Thank you, not today", my sister kept repeating forcibly, as we dashed up and down the alleyways, afraid to look sideways in case we had bought a roll of carpet or a barrel of tomatoes by mistake.

We turned a corner and found ourselves in the area where they sold spices. These smells were different, much stronger in a nicer kind of way. We discovered they were selling cumin seeds, coriander seeds, nutmegs, by the ton.

Hundred weight bags of cinnamon, ginger, WOW ! It was overpowering. By then, we had become more venturesome and my sister really wanted to buy about four ounces of saffron, which we knew would cost an arm and a leg at home, but the man insisted she buy a kilo. All I could think of was "Pam, please don't ! We'll get jail at the at the airport. They'll think it's drugs !" Come on Sis, time to run again.

The alleys seem to crisscross each other and everywhere seemed to be besieged with dark-eyed children asking for "Baksheesh" (money). We had crossed so many little streets that we were completely lost ! We tried to remember the different stalls, busy with craftsmen making the most beautiful leather handbags, tooled with gold and breathtaking handmade jewellery. The noise of the men and children making and hammering the bright copper jugs and household things was deafening but fascinating to watch.

My sister tried to barter for a beautiful cashmere shawl, all the shades between pale turquoise and dark green. Its touch was like pure silk, the wee beardy dark coloured man was asking a ridiculous price and he was insisting on draping it sensuously over her shoulder. She tried to tell him it was far too dear, she was only a poor woman from County Down ------ outer space to him ! He kept getting closer, leering and breathing his garlic breath all over us. Then he said he would give three camels to her husband if she came to live with him and she could have the shawl for free, or five camels if he could have me too ! Lucky old Alan ----- Imagine if he was rid of us and had five camels at Pacolet !! Deal or no deal ? OK Sis, run for it again !!

    At the next crossroads we seemed to have entered the fast food area. Everywhere there were gas burners, tended by little more than children. They seemed to be cooking all kinds of weird and wonderful food ------ if you dared eat it ! We slowed our pace, silly us ! From all sides, people kept pointing daggers with bits of barbequed meat on the end, expecting us to taste. We didn't dare enquire what the meat was. I must admit some of it smelled delicious. Yes, I did try some chargrilled lamb and it really was ! If only they hadn't made such a fuss, I might have tried some more. Didn't fancy the mint tea in those funny little cups much, I bet they never wash them out between customers ------ can't be too careful, you know !

    Time was moving on and we hadn't a clue where we were. It's funny that we never saw any of our fellow travellers. There were mostly dark-skinned men in long dirty white robes, some chewing awful red stuff called Betel Nut someone told us later, which they spat out now and again with great accuracy. The women were colourful but seemed to keep a low profile, and were low in numbers. We did manage to buy some of the wonderful blue-glazed pottery for which Tunisia is famous and some of their beautiful lace work, thanks to our courier's help who we had spotted buying the same.

    Now which way do we go ? Right or left, it all looked the same, crowds, colour, exotic smells ------- that's what

Souk means to me now. We made our decision, left it was. Our pace had now somewhat slowed, and although we tried to avoid eye contact, vendors still accosted us. The carpets seemed to be familiar, near where we came in a lifetime ago. There were rows and rows of carpets hanging up outside little shops at the perimeter wall. By now we were brave enough to look inside, if there was no one looking out at us ! Just as we were looking at a particularly beautiful carpet we became aware of a big Arab in his white head dress and robes appearing from somewhere, who seemed to be following us. We moved along very quickly and still he was there ! When the exit was in sight and there were still several carpet shops to pass, he suddenly approached us. "Lovelly Laideeeees, lovely ladieeeees ! You come to my shop, you buy my lovely carpets, I give you tea. I will take you home with me, I marry you ! Lovely Laideeeee, I make you good price !" He grabbed both of us by the arm and propelled us towards an empty shop. I nearly died of fright, and I know my sister was about to knee him in the you-know-where, when he let us go and said, in a broad Ulster accent, "Sure ye could buy it cheaper in Kilkeel anyway" !!! He was one of the men on our tour and he had bought himself a full Arab outfit for his golf club's annual fancy dress ball in Lisburn !

Two very relieved ladies made a beeline for the bus. We really needed our two very large gin and tonic's before dinner that night !! "Sousse and Souk ------ how are ye !"

Icelandic Ash and After

(Memories from the Inner Wheel Convention, Bournemouth "Rotary Club" ----- travelling with Nuala Osbourne and Elizabeth Hamilton)

Elizabeth was already in the bathroom, warbling in the shower, I was still warm and comfortable, basking in the sun on a tropical island when all Hell broke loose. Our 4.15 am wake-up call had come through, in triplicate from different parts of the room ! Different ringing tones ------ VERY, VERY LOUD !! I reached out and killed my mobile, then there were two ! The hotel phone was across the room beside my roommate's bed and God knows where she had kept her mobile at night. I leapt out of bed, strangled the hotel phone and still there was one left ! Found it, but it would not shut up ----- a good squeeze throttled it. Elizabeth appeared, all sparkling clean and hadn't heard a thing. My turn in the bathroom next and from there on the new day went rapidly downhill.

    With a final look around the bathroom and bedroom to check that no bits of us were left behind, we grabbed our baggage, coats, handbags and scuttled down the long corridor of the Royal Bath Hotel to the lift. It took us up to unknown heights before zooming us down to the depths of the building twice, before finally giving in and depositing us at ground floor and reception. Our taxi was booked for 5 am and as we walked towards reception we noticed several Inner Wheelers already in the dining room, having ordered an early breakfast ------ had they stayed up all night ? Chatting to them briefly, we indulged in a cuppa without sitting down and then made a beeline for the entrance hall. Taxi was waiting and we made the airport terminal in no time at all. Had our passports and boarding cards at the ready and checked in our bags at the desk, we were so organized Mr. Ryanair would have been proud of us ! Several others of the Irish contingent were checking in at the same time.

Nuala's case was a little overweight so she was trying to quickly off-load some stuff out of it into her cabin bag when we caught up with her. In went the black makeup zipper, along with other bits and this time the big suitcase was accepted. We went through security OK but then discovered Nuala had been detained, her cabin bag with the extra weight in it was the problem. Without much apology, the charming man was dumping all the forbidden liquids, good makeup, expensive perfumes, etc. He did offer to have her moisturiser analysed but she said, "Keep the feckin' lot !" Not a happy chick was she !

We joined the boarding queue for Dublin when called and proceeded out to the aircraft, only to stand in the freezing early morning cold on the tarmac for a good ten minutes, before the Ryanair staff would allow us move further towards the plane. Mind you, we did think it a bit peculiar when we spotted a mechanic under the belly of the plane opening flaps and examining the insides with a great big torch. "Oh well, it must be OK, doesn't look as if he has found a bomb."

Eventually, the very nice hostess told us we could board and we settled happily in our seats (priority boarding, much good did it do us !) At least we were aboard, warm, dry and belted in. A few minutes before take-off our Captain's voice came over the intercom, just to wish us a pleasant flight we thought. "Excuse me, what was that he said ? ------- I didn't quite catch ------", we all looked at each other in amazement. "This is your Captain speaking. On behalf of Ryanair I regret to inform you that something beyond our control has happened. A volcano has erupted in Iceland and all aircraft are being grounded. I have to ask you to disembark, taking your personal belongings with you and collect your luggage at the carousel. Thank you."

Well, amid loud talk of "Where's Iceland from here ?" and "What the Hell is O'Leary going to charge us for next ?" we got off and made our way back into the terminal. Staff seemed to be in a tizzy, so no one could give us any information about the next flight out, so we followed the crowd, collected our luggage and decided to taxi back into town.

Passing the Connaught Hotel, where Elizabeth and I had spent the Sunday night very comfortably before transferring to the conference hotel on Monday morning, we thought it might be a good idea to see if they could take us that night, in case we had to stay over, at least we'd have somewhere to stay. Nuala had joined with us so now we were three. The hotel was quite busy, as there seemed to be lots of folk staying on holiday. It was the last weekend before schools went back after the Easter holiday, and the weather was dry and sunny. Sorry, they had no single rooms left but we could have a family room. Great, we'll have it, thanks. We knew we'd be well looked after and the food was good. Problem solved !

What now ? It was still only around 7 am so coffee, a rest after the hassle and a combined think about the next move was in order. The sun was shining, some guests were heading for an early breakfast but bacon and eggs didn't appeal to us at all. After a while sitting in the lounge relaxing, a little elderly Indian lady, whose husband was paying their bill and checking out, came over and sat beside Elizabeth. She was full of chat and soon made it clear that she knew we were in some kind of difficulty. She started to give Elizabeth a lecture on how to handle stress, how to avoid it and the damage it does to one's health. She was rather domineering, in fact, terrifying ! She meant well, but we took a fit of the giggles and were highly relieved when her husband came to retrieve her. That was the first of our interesting encounters with strangers, in spite of what our mothers had told us years ago !

Left our luggage at the hotel, another taxi ride took us to the bus and railway terminal, there we caught up with the group from Omagh. After a confrontation with a very bolshy transport inspector, who was insisting that Bournemouth Airport had got it all wrong, the Omagh group decided to head for London. We were undecided and thought we'd try a travel agent. We came unstuck there too, no help at all ! Back to the train terminal we went and the wee man in the ticket office could not have been more helpful. He could book us through to Holyhead alright, but could not get us ferry tickets as the computers were down, warning us that the ferry would be packed with all the cancellations from the English airports. He said he would provisionally reserve three train tickets for us, but let him know if we made other arrangements, told us to go off and have a think about it.

Definitely time for food, so we headed to Dingles 5th floor restaurant. Lo and behold, there were the Lisburn group of Inner Wheelers, District Chairman Norma included, having lunch. They seemed to know what they were doing, Jane had the situation under control. We found a table next to them and then Elizabeth had a think-outside-of-the-box moment. She phoned her husband and asked him to phone their friend who knows about these things. The friend called her back, got the details and had us all fixed up with Travelodge accommodation and tickets for Stena Line ferry to Dublin port in no time at all !

There was a couple sitting next to us and they were fascinated by all the to-ing and fro-ing between us and all the mobile phone calls, we were the cabaret. The gentleman was very elderly and his companion was much younger.

(Daughter ? Could be maybe not, daughter would've helped him cut his meat up. We're not nosey, just interested !) It turned out she had been his secretary for nearly fifty years ! They go out for lunch once a month, usually to the same place. He had been in the Rotary and being in the company of so many Inner Wheelers made his day. "Wait till I tell the boys !" he told us. He must have been over ninety and still had a twinkle in his eye !!

Back we went to our nice wee man at the train ticket office. He suggested we sign up for the senior rail ticket and that would lessen the price of the journey, leaving it seventy-eight pounds. We took his advice and now we can travel on all the trains, provided we are back in England within the year, if we want to ! It took quite a while for him to do all the documentation for the three of us, however we were delighted to have it all sorted. We smiled and apologised to the first of a large queue that had formed patiently behind us and skedaddled quickly past them. Taxied back to the hotel feeling pleased with ourselves, settled in our room with a large drink to celebrate. We really enjoyed the superb dinner that evening and the same handsome French waiter with his efficient Hungarian waitresses remembered us from our previous stay. Three tired Inner Wheelers relaxed and had a good night's sleep not knowing there was lots more hassle to come.

A gentle start to the day, breakfast over at a very civilised hour, it was time for us to check out and reception called a taxi for us. We had plenty of time at the station to observe the action and people watch. There seemed to be an awful lot of very stylish folk on the opposite platform. Well tanned ladies in strapless summer dresses and killer heels despite the arctic wind and chilly sun, trendy guys with cameras. Something seemed about to happen. Then a sleek-looking train pulled in, there seemed to be about four long dining carriages with white tablecloths and table lamps at every window. We asked one of the rail staff what it was and he said, "Oh, that's the Orient Express." Apparently, you can book it for weddings or conferences. Maybe we could make a suggestion ? That was something we hadn't seen before.

Our train for Manchester/Piccadilly arrived on time and we jumped on, stored our luggage in the designated area and found our reserved seats a couple of rows away. I hadn't realised that the distances in England were so great and it would take seven hours to get to Holyhead from Bournemouth. We were just fine, our wee man had reserved seats with a table for us and it would be quite some time before we had to change at Wolverhampton. The trolley came around, we had coffee and sandwiches, sat back and enjoyed the scenery. Very pleasant indeed, we should go by train more often ------ if we had more trains !

After a while we noticed that the train had got much busier and soon there were a lot of people standing. Coming up to the Birmingham Exhibition Centre and Birmingham New Street Station the place was bunged with passengers. About half an hour from Wolverhampton, Elizabeth decided to visit the loo which was situated past the luggage racks and into the next carriage. When passing the luggage, she couldn't see her big black holdall, there were still people standing so coming past again she started to have a better look. A very kind man helped her move luggage to check everywhere but there was no sign of it. Nuala rushed to the opposite end of the train to find security personnel for her. I stayed put, guarding the rest of our belongings. Two security men came quickly and interviewed her but her bag could not be found. Luckily, she did not have credit cards or money in it for within a few minutes we were arriving at Wolverhampton station where we had to get off. There's nothing like a crisis when travelling to shake your confidence and boy, were we all shook up !

Elizabeth started to think about all that she had lost. "Oh, my God !! There's this ----- and that ----- and my ----- and the three lovely new pairs of shoes that I bought in Russell and ----- the purple beads I bought last week and all the good gear I had for the convention, never mind the fancy black holdall I bought for a bargain in TK Maxx. I should have brought my old beaten up one." We felt so sorry for her but not a thing we could do.

At Wolverhampton, we had to climb unending stairs over the bridge to the platform on the other side. We struggled up while passengers flew past us but some thoughtful young men offered to help, much appreciated and restored our faith in young people, so often maligned. Help the aged took on a new meaning, thanks boys !

On to the next packed train, seats booked but where ? We were not letting any luggage out of our sight. We flopped down on the first seats we could find. About three stops down the line the train came to a standstill. "Everybody off please, this train has broken down. Please board the train on Platform 3 to continue your journey." Oh Hell, where's Platform 3 ? Over more bloody stairs ! (Notice the cool has gone ?) Once again, nice young folk came to our rescue and we boarded a rickety basic train but gladly. This was packed too and was taking us to places we had never heard of, never mind pronounce. Ever heard that old Country and Western song, "I've Been Everywhere, Man" ? It goes off into a list of place names a mile long. Well, that's how it was for us:

"I've been everywhere, man, I've been to,

Bournemouth, Basingstoke, Southampton,

Oxford, Banbury, Coventry, Birmingham,

"Brummie" New Street, Coventry, Wolverhampton,

Shrewsbury, Newbury, Chester (and change),

Flint, Prestatyn, Rhyl and Pensarn,

Wrexham, Wreesam, Cyffredinol,

Oh, I've been everywhere, man,

Doesn't do no harm, man,

Abergele, Colwyn Bay, Bangor,

Someplace ending in red,

And over the Menai bridge to Holyhead."

     Holyhead, is it for real ? Must be, everyone's getting off. There were a few business men looking for taxis but not one in sight. Eventually two arrived together and the men commandeered one each. The taxi guy told us there'd be another along in a few minutes. There was a very nice young girl trying to get home to Cork (she'd come from London). She was telling us accommodation was impossible to find and that we were lucky to have a booking. She had tried for hours on the internet and all she could find was a farmhouse bed and breakfast miles away from Holyhead. We asked if she would like to share our taxi when it came along. We were happy to pay for it, thinking of our own daughters travelling in difficult circumstances but she turned the tables on us, insisting on paying, as she has a had a high-profile job in London and would be putting it down to expenses. She looked about sixteen ----- young people, they're great. Maybe she was thinking of her Granny !

     The Travelodge was nearby and there was a reservation for us, the receptionist told us she did not have a free room since the previous afternoon, the whole place had gone mad. No flights from anywhere and the ferries were filled to capacity. We were so lucky Elizabeth's plan worked ! While we were waiting to check in she must have dealt with five or six calls looking for accommodation. Later we asked her to recommend somewhere to eat as they did not serve food. She suggested a pub restaurant which turned out to be a £14 taxi ride out to the sticks. It was a very busy spot, popular with the locals, lots of Welsh spoken, good solid food with plenty of chips, beer and Friday night is karaoke night. Peaceful and quiet it was not. Back home to bed and the unsettling sight of families with children being turned away.

Next morning was bright and sunny again and as the Travelodge did not provide breakfast, we thought we'd go over to the ferry terminal early and have something there. Everyone we spoke to said it was only a very short distance ------ ten minutes at most. So we set off trundling our cases on wheels. The big bridge we were told to cross spanned the railway and led to the ferry terminal. It looked a very short distance but now it seemed to be getting further away. We plodded on manfully like Brown's cows, one behind the other on the narrow footpath.

Eventually, on coming to the base of this large silver bridge there seemed to be no way over it. Surely there must be a lift somewhere, certainly none was obvious. By this time some of us were buckling at the knees (me !). There was not much activity or people around, as it was hours before the ferry was due in and any traffic seemed to be commercial. We looked up in dismay, there was about six flights of stairs with at least twenty steps on each flight. As we stood looking up at this huge bridge, a bright young couple came jogging towards us. Elizabeth accosted them ----- "Excuse me, excuse me !" she said slowly, in her best Northern Ireland accent, (after all, they could have been Polish, Latvian or Welsh-speaking nationals !) "How do we get over the bridge ? Is there an elevator ?" They stopped, looked at one another and you knew they were thinking, we've a right lot here ! "You want to cross the bridge ?" the guy said, "OK, let me help you." And with that he picked up Nuala's big heavy bag, my smaller but weighty one and Elizabeth's remaining cabin bag and bounded off up the stairway ! Grateful thanks to our unknown Good Samaritan.

Safely in the terminal coffee shop building and with the necessary refreshments, Elizabeth got in contact with the travel police to report her loss. She had been told by the security men on the train to inform them too. A very sympathetic lady cop came over and took a list of everything Elizabeth could remember. By now the crowds were beginning to arrive and the lady cop's male counterpart came over to tell her that the lunacy was beginning. We didn't know what he meant then but we were soon to find out. Our crowd, who had already had reservations, formed a short queue at the entrance barrier to the Dublin ferry. Hordes of people, disembarking from the boat which had just docked, were starting to pour out from another entrance into the same area. They were panicking to buy train tickets to get out of Holyhead, and another queue, which was tripling by the minute were panicking to buy tickets for the ferry. Lunacy was the word for it !!

We had managed to work our way to the front of the queue, by fair means or foul, and just stood there. Eventually a man lifted the barrier and as the crowd surged forward, boy did we beat the posse, only trouble was we didn't know where to go ! Two of the Stena personnel told us to head for the rows of busses taking passengers to Dublin city but we didn't want to go there, only to the port, as the husbands were collecting us there. Sheer bedlam ! There we were standing in this transit shed, with hundreds of people rushing headlong past us to the busses and we, who had been there all morning, were being left behind !! After some time and a lot of worry by us, a bus came along to take the remaining passengers who were only going to the port to the boat. Needless to say, there was hardly a vacant seat on the boat !

Poor Nuala just wanted to go home to Sligo but her family had other ideas. There was to be a big family reunion at a posh hotel in Kildare that night and after many phone calls, it was arranged that her daughter would pick her up at Dublin Port. (How did we manage before mobiles were invented ?) "I've no makeup, my clothes are all creased and I'm jaded," Nuala's pleas went unheeded. "You'll be fine after the hairdo and facial we've arranged for you at the hotel ----- we couldn't do without you, Mum !" I hope she had a super night.

The boat docked and again, we were last to leave. As we got into the lift to go down to ground level, Nuala disappeared with her heavy case. Elizabeth and I stopped the lift at each level but no sign of Nuala among the queues of people going down the stairs to their vehicles. We went up and down a few times and every time the door opened the same faces were staring at us. They didn't seem amused, everyone was hot and flustered, and not a sign of her anywhere. "Well, she's a big girl now and she'll hardly get lost in Dublin", we thought. Before we knew it we were outside and there was Nuala complete with her luggage ! A quick look around and there were the relieved husbands coming to greet us, delight on all our faces ! With the brief introductions over, Nuala's daughter whisked her off to the delights of Kildare and we were whisked off to delightful Rostrevor.

Cash Only

Cash ! Oh yes, I'd need some of the "readies". That dates me, fine, I'm of the age where I don't offer my credit card to the shopkeeper for only a newspaper or a pint of milk ! By the time I remembered that I needed cash, I'd just driven past the bank and noticed there was one empty disabled parking space outside it, which the car on my tail slipped into ------ OK, round the block I go, back past the bank again and not a parking place in sight, disabled or otherwise. Now, you younger people, there comes a time when you will need to get as near to the place you are going to as possible ! If walking is slow, get yourself a blue badge, it sure beats a long walk from the town car park ! On the third lap round I was lucky, a man in his large BMW pulled out and I was able to slip into his designated blue badge space.

    Right, OK, good so far ------ retrieved my blue badge from the driver's door pocket to place it in a prominent position, photo side down, on the dashboard in front of the windscreen. I set it on the passenger seat for a moment until I find the bank card for the ATM machine, it's safely somewhere in my big handbag, with its many compartments. Great, there's nobody in the queue for the machine. I know the bank card is in there somewhere. Oh look, there's the birthday card I meant to post yesterday ! Found the card, handbag over arm, walking stick at the ready, keys of the car in hand. Alight from car, lock it, turn around, lo and behold

you, there is a queue of three customers for the ATM ! -------
I mutter a BAD word that I didn't think I knew and it wasn't
"Oh deary, deary me" !

    I stand and patiently wait my turn, no problem, deed done, with money and receipt tucked safely in the bag. Perhaps I should go to the post office while I'm here, post the birthday card and buy some extra stamps. Very, very short walk to the post office. Queue up again, behind several people. The old fellow at the counter must be buying the post office, he is taking so long and there's only two assistants on duty.

    I DON'T BELIEVE IT ! The second assistant has eventually finished with her customer and taken herself off to the room behind the office. Number one assistant is still dealing with the difficult old boy who is hard of hearing and he is not giving up easily. He keeps asking the girl questions which she has to look up in a big book and he is not satisfied with her answers. "Please please, come on ! I only want a book of stamps", I moan inwardly. There's still two ladies in front of me and several people have joined the queue behind us. I can see three positions behind the counter for staff and there's not one in any of them. Assistant number two returns from the back office, has a word or two with the girl who is coping with the difficult man, returns to her position and with a big smile beckons the next customer.

    Eventually it's my turn, "A book of second-class stamps and put one on this card, please." The girl smiles,

"Just pop it on the scales for me please, it's not a regular size." I do as I'm told and push it over the counter to her. She stops, looks at the envelope and then at me in amazement, "I can't accept this without a postcode", she says ----- (Holy crow ! The full name and proper address is on it, I know, I've checked it). "Sorry, you need a postcode", she says again with a smile. "How do I find that ?" I ask. She gives me her big warm smile again, "I can look it up for you, but it will take me a minute or two, we're quite busy this morning." I give her permission, stand at the counter and wait, same as the old boy at the next booth with number one assistant, acutely aware of the hostile stares of the queueing customers, while she disappears again into that back office. After a long minute or two, she's back, found the elusive postcode and stamped the envelope. I thank her, pay quickly and skedaddle past the queue as fast as the gammy knee will let me.

Perhaps I should buy the local newspaper, just next door, while I am here. I pick up the paper and a magazine, make my way to the checkout. Goodness me, haven't magazines become expensive and sure there's nothing in them only adverts ! Anyway, back to the car now, home and a nice hot cuppa would be good. Hello, hello ! What is he doing pacing round my car in his red coat and peaked cap ? I'm perfectly parked in the disabled spot, between the lines and not touching the kerb or cars.

"Your vehicle Madame ?" "Yes", I replied icily. "You know you're not allowed to park here, these spaces are reserved for people who are disabled" he growled at me, with a look of disgust on his face. "If you look you will see that indeed I have a blue badge in place on the dash. I admit my mobility is not great and I'm not using my walking stick", I kept to my icy tone. "Where, Madame, is your badge ? I don't see any on display." He stood holding his wee book and his pencil, poised in a most menacing way. Sure enough, there was no badge on view. Oh flip, what did I do with it ? I looked into the car and there it was sitting on the passenger seat, just where I had left it. Peaked cap was not happy. I was not happy. "Oh look !" I said, "It must have fallen off the dash. Maybe the vibration of a big lorry dislodged it." (In a quiet one way street, with not much heavy traffic ?) Isn't it funny how, at times, the most unlikely story can come innocently out of your mouth with no warning ! He looked at me for a while and then growled, "At least you have one, I hope it's in date and make sure you display it where it can be seen !" and off he stomped hoping to find some other unfortunate offender.

    My luck seemed to change, maybe the encounter with the red coat was lucky after all. Coming out of town, on the way home there's a long straight stretch of road with a 40 mph speed restriction on it, where there's hardly a house in sight. Although I have heard of speed cops occasionally being seen there, I, and hundreds like me, sail along there frequently with hardly a thought of acceptable speed. Well, when two approaching cars flashed their lights at me, I took their advice, slowed down and dandered along at 25 mph, smiled, blew a kiss and cheerily waved a salute at the big checkered white van carefully parked in a disused gateway with an uninterrupted view of passing traffic !!

Home safe and boy, did that cup of tea taste good !

Not Her Again !

Hello. Hello there. Great to see you ! My goodness, YOU'RE looking well ! I meant to phone you after I heard that your cousin, what's his name ------ died last year, but I just never got round to it. Sorry about that !

I saw ------ you know, emmm ----- your sister-in-law, the one that's married to your oldest brother, Jim ----- or is it John, in a supermarket the other day in Newry ----- or was it Rathfriland ? I think it was Rathfriland. Anyway, it was a very wet day and she seemed to be in an awful rush, so I didn't get a chance to chat to her but she waved over at me and hurried on out just as I was going over to speak to her. She's looking great. I suppose she has more time to herself now that the family have grown up.

I heard that one of the sons got married, what's this they called him ? No, no, not the wee black-haired one that looks so like his Daddy, the other one. Definitely, there's a great likeness to, emmm ------ her ones. Didn't he marry the wee girl who always walked the two big dogs ? What's this they called her ? Wasn't she one of the big family that lived on the corner of Brookvale ----- or was it Riverdale ? Sure it had to do with water anyway ! The father was a big tall man, I think he worked in the bank ----- or maybe it was insurance. A far-out cousin of ours, but I can't remember which one, would be a relation of hers, I think.

My goodness, hasn't the town changed since we were running about ! Do you ever see or hear from ----- you know, the nice girl who worked in ----- where was it ? They stocked ----- Och, you remember the colour of tights we couldn't buy in the other shop, where the manageress was called ------ sure, I forget her name too ----- was it Vera ? No, no, not her, the big elderly cross one who was always giving off about something. You used to be very friendly with that nice wee girl. I don't think that shop is there any more, or was it closed down ?

What about your own sister ? I forget her name ----- the tall one, I suppose she's married with a grown family. Who's this she married ? When she was young she used to do a great line with ----- do you remember the good-looking big fella, what's his name ----- with the fancy sports car who worked in Banbridge or Belfast, or was it his mate ----- who always wore the Aran sweater, whatever you called him. Oh, she married HIM ? Thought she'd have married the good-looking one ! Ahh well, sure looks aren't everything.

I suppose your Aunt, Mrs. ------ what's her name, is still alive ? She must be a big age by now, is she still living on her own in that nice house, down the road in the new development with the funny name ? ----- I can never remember what you call it.

Better get this shopping finished and get away home before dark. Great to see you again, be sure and tell the rest of them I was asking for them. Bye now !

Now who on earth was that woman I was just talking to ? I know the face but for the life of me, I can't think of her name !

Mind the No Parking Sign

Go and pour yourself a cup of coffee and I'll tell you what happened to me today in Lisburn. I am quite old now, mobility not so great even with the walking stick. I had some business to do at an office in Market Place, and of course not a free parking space, for disabled blue badge holders or otherwise. I found one around the corner, less than two-minutes' walk away (at my speed) and parked in it. Here was my mistake, I had set my blue badge on the passenger seat while I gathered up my handbag, necessary papers and walking stick but forgot to put it up on the windscreen !

    About three minutes later I was back, the office had closed ten minutes earlier at four o'clock ! Lo and behold, this wee beardy man in uniform was on standby, writing me a parking ticket ! He obviously hadn't looked into the car, it was just not my day. He was quite unfriendly and my goodness when I opened his note it was a fine for ninety pounds !! ----- I did have the blue badge and actually my new one arrived a day or two previous, but hadn't made it as far as my car yet, so now I have two. The wee man said to photocopy my blue badge and send it with the summons into headquarters.

    So here goes. I'll send copies of both, in case another wee man says the first one is out of date ! I won't make the same mistake again.

Enjoy your coffee, because someday you'll be old too and a bit forgetful ----- it's not that funny ! Best wishes and as they say, "Have a nice day !"

Wee John

Good grief !! Am I THAT old ? Saw an obituary in today's newspaper of a wee fellow I used to play with. Yep, I've read obituaries of folk whom I knew before but this one really shook me. Wee John was a right nuisance when we were playing games at our seaside holiday homes in Killowen Point, always getting in the middle of things that he had no need to be involved in. With his skinny wee legs, well-worn shorts, much-loved Fair Isle jumper and a perpetual runny nose.

 He had a protective older brother Jim, who was our age, great fun and we didn't want to fall out with him. Jim had quite a few brothers and sisters, but Wee John was always the fly in the ointment. Not that he was really bad ! He just had the knack of making a nuisance of himself or causing things to go wrong ! You know the kind of child, the one who wants to damage the best football in the middle of a game to see what kind of leather it's made from, punctures it or kicks it into the sea by mistake, or throws a stone which goes through Mrs. What's-her-name's window and gets us all chased from playing in the field next to her house.

 Wee John came from a large family, the children were all good playmates except him, because we never knew what would happen next if he was on our team ! He was always asking questions, "Why is that ------ ?" "What's that for ?" and mostly, "Ahh, but what if ----- ?" We didn't know the answers. Silly us.

I remember hearing in our recently grown-up years that Wee John was doing awfully well at University ------- University ? Wee John ? Life goes on, we were all busy with our own problems, careers, marriage, children, health but now and then, thoughts go back to those carefree days at Killowen Point when we swam, caught eels under the stones when the tide was out and didn't want Wee John to be on our team !

Today's newspaper tells me of Wee John's death. A half-page relating the life and achievements of a highly respected and prominent member of university life in Dublin, Professor of Chemical Engineering, Professor Emeritus. Imagine that !! Wee John ! How I wish we had tried to find answers to his many questions.

Rest in peace Wee John.

Pup's Song

Ever heard Johnny Cash sing "A Boy Named Sue" ? In cat terms that's me, only they call me Pup ! ------ Pup ? I ask you ------ where did they get that from ? You'd think they'd know the difference between cats and dogs ! Ahh sure, if it makes them happy, it makes me happy too !

    Last year, I was born into a homeless one parent family up on the hill. My old man had scarpered and Mum was left with us. Mum was good-looking, promiscuous and savvy. She wanted only the very best for us. She told us we were beautiful and descended from a breed called Maine Coon. American, she thought, maybe that's why she always miaowed with an American accent ! True, I've inherited the long body, white socks, white belly and the stripy tail but I honestly think by the time the genes got down our length, and with Mum's lifestyle, the breed's distinctive features had watered down a bit !

    Mum sussed out the neighbourhood, looking for likely adoptive clients with suitable accommodation and no other animals in residence. She found one and at the earliest she could safely abandon me, dropped me in the flowerbed at their back door when they were out. When the folks returned (ancient man and wife), the wife went out again immediately ----- think she forgot to get milk or something. That was my cue, I miaowed loudly, Boss-man came out and found me. He had left the door open, so I shot into the house and hid under the sideboard. He lay down on the floor with a piece of cake to entice me out, yuk ! Boss-woman returned and nearly had hysterics when she saw him prone on the floor ! If I had known he had been poorly I'd have jumped up on something higher like the curtains !

    All he could say was, "Guess what ? We've got a cat !" I didn't know they were dog lovers and never had a cat before. Apparently, over the years they'd always had dogs, in fact they had many, but they lived near a busy road. After the last dearly loved casualty had departed to chase cars in the sky, there were no more dogs. Oh, it doesn't bear thinking about ------- Hadn't they a big enough garden to play in ? Now does it make sense ?

    Come, Pup ------ here's your favourite tuna supper. Oh, you are the most beautiful Pup. Are you warm enough ? Come up on the sofa beside me for a cuddle. Can't you hear me purr ? Wow, it's a Pup's life, so far !

P.S. Feel I should check out the night life more around here, although I know they don't agree with my staying out late, in case I get into bad company. Anyway, I can't stay in every night, a girl's got to do what a girl's got to do. Tonight, I'll head up the country under the bridge so I won't have to cross that busy road. Traffic is dangerous, cars don't stop for cats, you know ! No moon, tall shadows, dark fields, wet grass, black hedges, dense undergrowth, no light, strange smells, sinister noises !

Oh, oh, oh !!! ------ There's big trouble coming, sorry folks ! ------ Over and out quickly. (Thanks Gladys, for breaking the news !)

Cat's Cradle

Well, like them or loathe them ------ take your pick ! My husband was never a cat enthusiast. In fact, he just didn't like them because they chased the wee birds in the garden, he much preferred dogs and so did I.

When he first became ill, a tiny kitten appeared from nowhere at our back door one day and he brought it into the house. Very shortly, it had won him over and they became inseparable. No bad thing I thought, because dog walking days were over for both of us. So that's how Pup (the kitten) got her name. Pup was very much my husband's companion, she was in residence with us for nearly a year and then wanderlust got her. Maybe she got fed up with us, she went off one night and never came home. We kept hoping she'd turn up but she never did.

After a few months, the house seemed lonely with neither a dog or cat to create a diversion for the old pair. So one day, on a curiosity mission to the local USPCA, I thought I'd drop in and see what there was on offer. They had quite a few dogs, two lovely collies needing rehomed but a bit big for us and, I'd say, needing a lot of exercising ------ that's them off the list for us, unfortunately !

Around the corner, in a different area was a pen of kittens, at least ten, if they stayed still long enough to count ! I watched them for quite a while and boy, were they having fun tumbling over each other, stalking each other, jumping over the boxes and things put into their pen to stimulate play. I noticed two little ones, sitting on a big box quietly watching the others. One was white and tan, the other was white, tan and dark brown.

Emmm, I thought, I wonder how one of those would fit into our routine. I had a word with the girl at the desk, she came with me to look, told me one was spoken for but the other was for rehoming. I thought this poor kitten was going to be left on its own and it would probably break its wee heart ! Maybe I should do something about it. I offered to take it home right away, but the girl said that was not their policy. I would have to think it over, be really sure and come back to answer a few questions in a day or two, before any animal could leave to go to a new home. Fair enough, I thought, maybe I should inform the husband first. I didn't bother !

Two days later, I headed back to the complex, found the surplus kitty sitting on its own, looking sad, completely ignoring the complicated games the others were playing. The girl I had been speaking with the day before wasn't there, but a big friendly young man took us (the kitten and I) under his care. Ended up I had to buy a cat travel cage, special kitten food, a cat bed and cat litter and give a donation to the charity. Well, all this was new to me, as our only other kitten didn't cost us a penny because she had found us ! "In for a penny, in for a pound" I thought, and drove home wondering what on earth had come over me.

Pip, as we decided to call her, naturally was a bit overwhelmed. When I brought her in to the living room, she immediately shot in behind the sofa and stayed there for two days ! No amount of coaxing to get her out worked. I had to lift her out, bring her outside to the old flower bed, wait and hope she had performed and bring her back in again, where she would just shoot under the sofa again.

The husband wasn't all that thrilled about it either, and it took a lot of coaxing to get him to even acknowledge there was a kitten in the house ! Eventually, Pip got a bit more used to us and was not so timid. She would jump up on my knee, cuddle down for a little while, but was easily disturbed by any noise and would immediately jump down to seek refuge behind the sofa. The husband and she were very wary of each other, he kept telling me that I should bring her back to the orphanage, as he didn't think she would ever settle ! There was just some animosity between them, she would stalk him walking up the corridor to the hall and pounce at his ankles ! Twice he accused her of attacking him when he was reading the paper, which I laughed at ! Until the third time, when I saw that she had scratched his hand, this time very deeply and we felt it was necessary to take him to A&E in case of infection.

Anyway, I think she didn't fancy going back to the "orphanage" and one evening she did a runner. We searched the local roads but there was no sign of an RTA (road traffic accident) !

Definitely no more cats ------ but guess what we've got now ? We have Mr. and Mrs. Robin who pop in regularly for a quick snack, give us a song and keep an eye on us. The blue tits have discovered the little bird house nailed to a tree at the bottom of the garden and a big thrush has taken to sitting on a fence near the window. So we are looking forward to welcoming in whole families, now that dogs or cats are no longer in residence.

Isolation, Insomnia and I (Me !)

The first few days were bliss ------ didn't do anything, apart from thinking about all the things I was going to do next week ------ if this isolation and the close down thing lasts !

It IS lasting ! Now all the shops have closed, except the food stores and pharmacies. Cafés, hotels and pubs are all locked up, that's impossible you'd think but it's for real !! Some factories are closed too ----- this is ridiculous ! I don't believe it !! People are told not to go to work, use the very reduced public transport, and if possible work from home ! That won't suit a lot of people, what will they do ? I listen to every news bulletin on the hour and things are not good ! The schools are closed now too, and hospitals won't allow visitors in to see sick relatives, even those who are dying ! How will people manage ? What is the world coming to ?

No social gatherings and all the big events cancelled, the annual agricultural show at Balmoral in Belfast, all the sports fixtures, just imagine ! No football matches anywhere, even the golf club's closed !! Stay indoors, keep safe, keep your distance, at least two metres apart ! Many airlines have closed down, no travel ----- it's scary ! Churches are closed, no services, no weddings, no christenings, no wakes, only 6 mourners or relatives allowed at funerals !! What on earth are we going to do ? How will we cope ? What will people do for money ? There's talk on the news that those who have lost their jobs will be on "furlough", meaning that the government will pay part of their wages !

Tomorrow, I'll just keep busy ------ I will clear out the kitchen drawers, reorganise all the cupboards, sort out the far too numerous dishes, tea and dinner services seldom used, downsize all the shelves of surplus towels, bedding and bathroom equipment, tackle the garage and that awful cupboard where I put things that might come in handy some day (the don't-dump-it-just-yet cupboard !) Then I will make a start on my wardrobe, ditch all the jackets and things that I haven't worn for at least two years and get myself up to date. Oh yes, there's going to be a "new me" after this is all over ! A week should do it ! I'll leave lots of stuff to the local charity shops. Oh heck, they're probably all closed too !

The news bulletins are depressing, so many confirmed cases of this dreaded Covid-19 virus, so many dead. Every news report brings more bad news. Keep in, keep safe, keep your distance ! The over seventies are vulnerable and must not go out or mix with people (Goodness, that's me ----- when did this happen, I hadn't noticed !) I can exercise a little daily by walking in the garden but I must isolate, stay indoors, close my door to all callers, wash my hands again and again, use disinfectant wipes on all the door handles, the house phones and any hard surfaces I might touch.

Good grief, there's only me in the house now ! One day merges into another and I have started to do many things but finished nothing ------- is this Thursday or Friday ? If it's Friday, then it's bin day but which bin do I leave out ?

There's very little in any of them and anyway it's too late now, it's 9 am, bet the bin lorry's long since gone. Ahh well, it'll do until next week.

Must wash the hands after touching anything that anyone else may have touched, sing "Happy Birthday to You" three times while washing with the special gel ------ that's the length of time it takes to wash the hands thoroughly (wonder who thought that one up !!) Dry with paper towel and dump it. Always use a hand sanitiser if washing is not available ! Wash your hands, keep safe, keep two metres distance from anyone else, is the mantra on television and radio !

Phone calls come in fast and furious the first few days, from long lost friends and relations, always the same questions, "How are you coping ?" and "I wonder how long will this last ?" Everyone's in the same boat, or as someone said, we're not all in the same boat but we're in the same storm ! No other half now, no dog, no cat, no callers at the door, no one to talk with in the house. I know I'm lucky having brief evening visits from family, who stay outside on the porch, drink coffee, have a chat through the open door, because some people are completely alone all day, having no immediate family around, and maybe living in a small apartment with no garden. Changed times indeed !!

Very little traffic passing by on the road, a few folks out walking, singly or keeping the stipulated two metres distance between each other. I watch from the window, cyclists zooming along, usually on their own, not in the groups we were always complaining about ! Joggers getting on with their serious exercise and moving out onto the road to pass pedestrians on the footpath. No stopping to chat, a friendly nod of the head and move on ! Thank goodness the weather is fine. The evenings are clear, there's time to sit with a coffee and watch the bird life on the beach from the window. I wonder what the names of some of them are, I hadn't realised there were so many different kinds, must get a good bird book next time I'm in town ------ Ooh, I wonder when that will be !!

 Relatives and friends kindly offer to do my shopping or get medical prescriptions for me, if needed. There's an air of helpfulness around, neighbours wave from their gardens and the elderly keep in touch by phone. The number of those who have contracted the disease keeps rising, and the number of deaths also rises on a daily rate, reported frequently on the media. The virus seems to affect mostly the elderly and those who have other health problems, although no one is really exempt. Keep in, keep safe, keep your distance ! They tell me there are queues at the food shops. You have to line up outside with a distance between each person, with a door man allowing entry on a one-in, one-out system !!

 Bed early these nights, comfortable with my books, nearly up to date magazines, the iPad and the BBC radio chat show, which is interspersed every few minutes with more depressing news of the Covid-19 virus. Sleep doesn't come easy now, the way it always did and the reading matter doesn't hold me the way it once did, thank goodness for the iPad ! I pass the time writing long emails to long lost relations in New Zealand and elsewhere, telling them of my woes. Looking up the latest information about the virus. Viewing property for sale, which I wouldn't buy even if I had the millions. Exotic holidays to places I've never even heard tell of. Even the obituary column (to make sure my name is not on it !) There goes one o'clock, three o'clock, four o'clock ------ Goodness, it will soon be daylight and I haven't closed an eye yet ! Wonder how many more weeks of this we'll have to put up with (please don't tell me). I talk to myself a lot these days, it's better than nobody and I can repeat myself as many times as I like !

My poor car doesn't understand why we are not going anywhere, most unusual and the petrol tank is nearly full ! I was afraid of the battery going flat after two weeks being stationary, so I did a runner (naughty !) Took the car out, did a fast drive to Kilkeel, not stopping anywhere and safely straight back home. It was weird, everywhere closed, just like a Sunday and only the tide went out, as Max Boyce wrote later in his poem about the unrealness of this time ! There's hardly anyone on the usually busy street, the shop windows are all shuttered.

I've started to bake bread and cakes, which I always enjoyed. It helps to pass the time, giving some to family when they come to check on me, but clearing out the cupboards has come to a complete standstill ! Ahh well, maybe tomorrow I'll feel more like it. I think I need company. We've always had dogs, in fact many dogs over the years, several being victims of road traffic accidents as we live near a busy road. The husband and youngest son were always the main dog walkers, enjoying hikes along the beach or up in the forest park. Yep, I'd love a dog but it would have to be walked every day, I don't think my gammy knee would allow that. Sorry about that. Even an old decrepit dog ? No dear, it would only get sick and you would have to take it to the vet, forget it. You are supposed to be isolated. How about a wee kitten then ? No, lovely as they are for a short time they tend to ramble, or maybe you'd trip and fall over it. You're one of the "vulnerable people" now remember ? You don't want to cause the hospital unnecessary work, they have enough to do with this Covid-19 crisis. No cats or kittens either, sorry ! There I go, talking to myself again !

Oh heck, I'm lonely ! I take a walk around the garden and spot many things needing attention. The sea comes right up to the garden wall, the garden is about twelve feet above the shoreline and we have a small concrete deck with steps down from the garden. There are two big seagulls sitting there quite comfortable, they don't move as I go over to the fence for a closer look. One gave a disdainful squawk, looked at the other one first, then looked up at me and the two of them flew off together. OK, did I do or say something ?

Next morning, the two seagulls were back sitting on the deck in the sunshine, as if they owned it. I threw them some stale bread, which they downed in five seconds, I went back into the house, brought them a little more and told them that was all I had. They seemed to understand and with another solitary squawk from one of them, they flew off. That evening they were back, standing on the deck looking up at the house. I had noticed one of them doing a close fly past the window a couple of times earlier. I took the hint and with a couple of leftover potatoes from dinner, went out to have a word with them. They were very grateful for the scraps, squawked their thanks again and flew off.

    I told myself that they are my new pets, better than a dog that would have to be walked, or a kitten that might wander away and get lost ! Now "Simon and Garfunkel" book in with me for breakfast and an evening meal most days. I've named them such because they are my "Bridge over Troubled Water" in these troubled times ! They are great company, don't have to be looked after and happily use up any leftover food. One does a fly past the kitchen window first, to let me know they are there, the other one just sits on the deck and waits for the food. After they have eaten, they always thank me before they fly off. We have great chats together, I'm learning the basics of "seagull squawk" but I always reply in my own language !!

    The family promise that they won't tell anyone that their mother has long meaningful conversations with two seagulls ! I do enjoy their company, it's lovely when they pop in to see me, stay a while and check how I am coping with isolation. Two loud cheerio squawks, "See you tomorrow" and then they're off. You know, I'm getting quite used to this sheltered life and the thought of busy shops and a more frantic life style is a bit scary ! My interest in the weather patterns and local wildlife as seen from the window has developed !

I notice there are very few vapour trails from airplanes in the clear blue sky these days and shipping is about a quarter of the usual amount going into the port. I notice the sea water is very clear, seaweed can be clearly seen growing underwater for quite a distance, wonder why ? Now that I think of it, the birds singing in the trees seems very loud, the dawn chorus sounds like a full blown orchestra for fifteen minutes at daybreak ! I'd never been awake to hear it before ! Maybe this necessary lockdown has shown us the possibility of a quieter lifestyle, time to reflect and appreciate the wonders of nature all around us.

Our Charlie's Story

I'm a wee black and white kitten, of no great aristocratic lineage but I do have a built-in awareness of humans with needs, some really profound and some just downright daft !

When I was really, really young, I lived in a nice old farmhouse with my Mum and two sisters. We weren't allowed into the big house of course, our home was in one of the many outhouses. Oh, it was warm, dry and comfortable enough. We slept on old bags in the corner and Missus What's-her-name who lived in the big house saw that we had enough milk and leftovers every day in a couple of old bowls, plenty for the four of us. No big deal for they had a few cows that had to be milked by Himself every evening in the byre, right next to our accommodation.

Mum was a good "mouser", so we were never short of a bit of beef. She would even have tackled a rat but I reckoned that was a bit dangerous and that she should just leave it to Winston the Jack Russell, who was a wild man, always on the lookout for a bit of sport. You could hear him bark a mile away, and visitors were always slow to get out of their cars because he would snap at their ankles. Jack Russells were bred to round up cattle you know, but sometimes he pretended he didn't know the difference between humans and cattle. Stupid dog !

We always kept a low profile when visitors or anyone

appeared in the yard. Mum had taught us to observe and be cautious of strangers, although if a child appeared wanting to pet us that was OK, we could purr as much as we liked and that would make them happy. Purring is a good exercise for cats and kittens, it's good for stress and makes a cat feel comfortable too. It's funny because even I (knowing a lot of things) don't know where the noise comes from, or how we make it !!

One morning, Mum heard the Missus saying to a friend who had dropped by for a coffee and chat, that they had far too many cats. Well, that was a bit of news alright, I didn't think four was too much for a place like this and neither did Mum. We wondered what was going to happen, and for another week nothing did.

On Tuesday, I think it was Tuesday, the Missus' friend arrived after lunchtime and they had a long conversation. Mum saw them coming out of the house and heading our way. My sisters and I were playing hide and seek in and out of two or three old empty cardboard boxes. Mum shot into the biggest box and we all followed her, bit of a squeeze but we cuddled in and waited. The ladies stopped at our door but her friend had spotted an unusual bush growing at the entrance to the old walled garden and off they went to examine it. The chit-chat went on and on, then they made their way on into the garden. Phew, we thought, bet the flowers and plants are more interesting than we are.

We had nearly forgotten about them when they

appeared back in our doorway. The Missus came in calling, "Come here Kitty, Kitty and bring your wee ones !" Mum came out of the box, arched her back, stretched, yawned and walked away from them, with her tail in the air. We (my sisters and I) weren't sure what to do, so we came out anyway, on the off chance they had some tidbits for us. The Missus picked the girls up in her arms and told her friend that these two young ladies would be available for adoption, preferably to the same household, they were fond of children and both were house-trained. Well, well ! Where did she get that from, I wondered. Sure none of us had ever been in a people house before ! The friend coooed over them and said she knew the perfect family who would just love to have them both ! The Missus carried them off towards the house and Himself appeared with a box with a lid on it, my sisters were dropped into it, then the friend put the box on the back seat of her car. Cheerio's were said, promises of phone calls of their arrival with the new family, off they went and that was the last I ever saw of my sisters.

So that just left Mum and me. I could see Mum had other things on her mind and she sort of ignored me for a few days. She seemed to go off hunting a lot and didn't appear home till evening. I was a bit fed up doing nothing, only chasing dead leaves blowing about in the yard and practicing the stalking skills that Mum had taught me.

A few days later the Boss-man dropped in to our outhouse to collect a few empty hessian bags and stopped to chat to me, first time he ever did that ! He said, "Young man,

I think I know of a lady who would be very good to you and happy to have a new man in her life to fuss over. How would you fancy living in a real house and keeping your eye on this old lady ?" ------ Well, that was a bit of a shock to me but what the heck, I thought, it sounds good. Just hope she would not be too bossy or have other live-in animals. I meowed that I would be happy to give it a go and if I didn't like it, I could always find my way back here with my built in sat-nav. A day or so later, I overheard that the daughter of the house had contacted the old lady who said she had no intention of having another dog or cat about the place. She'd been there, done that and got the tee-shirt enough times ! Talk about feeling rejected !

    One afternoon, the daughter (I'll call her "Sally") came to find me. She made a great fuss of me, squirted some liquid and rubbed it well into my coat, then gave me a good polish all over with a warm duster and a cuddle ------ Oh, it was bliss !! Before she left she put a crumbled up tablet into my supper, country bumpkin that I was I didn't know it was to kill any fleas and worms that I might have, but I did enjoy the cuddle !

    The next evening when Sally appeared at the door, Mum still wasn't home, in fact, she hadn't appeared home all night and I was really beginning to worry about her. Maybe she was worried about a young one like me not making any effort to move out to find a place of my own. Sally had a big basket with a lid, she scooped me up, dropped me into it and before I knew it I was on the back seat of her Jeep.

After about a twenty-minute drive we called at one of Sally's friend's houses and I was duly brought in for the family to admire this lovely wee kitten. I really didn't know how to handle this, so as I leapt out of Sally's arms I gave her a good scratch on the hand and hid behind the sofa. Yes yes, OK OK, I know, it was a stupid thing to do and it didn't show me in a good light, specially when Sally's friend said "Thank God that cat is not coming to this house !" I was mortified to see poor Sally stopping the blood with her hanky ! We didn't stay long, needless to say and we journeyed on to my unknown destination. I didn't know it at the time but that was the friend Sally was hoping would take me to live with her, as she was always saying how much she would love a puppy or a kitten, if the old lady turned me down.

We arrived at the house and the lady was delighted to see Sally. She lived on her own and with the Covid pandemic thing she'd had few visitors and was finding life quite lonely. After the welcome and a bit of chit-chat, Sally brought me in from the car to introduce me ----- saying that we intended to call with a friend who might be interested in giving me a home. I had learned a lesson at the other house, so I blinked my big eyes up at the lady when she tickled me under my chin and purred as loudly as I could !

I had good vibes about this house, it was warm and comfortable, the lady seemed kind and I couldn't detect any sign of other animals around. The other house was noisy, people were talking loudly and the television was on full blast (Remember, I had never been inside a people house, never mind seeing people talking inside a box in the corner of the room !) This seemed a much better proposition, quiet and warm. The lady took me in her arms, stroked my head and back and I felt relaxed. She said "Sally, what a lovely wee fella. Common sense tells me I don't want another cat but gosh, he's lovely !" They chatted on about things and people I didn't know or understand. The woman just kept stroking me, so I relaxed and purred as loudly as I could. Eventually, Sally said it was time to go as her Dad needed the Jeep. The lady was holding on to me and I made no effort to move. Sally laughed and said, "The pair of you look very comfortable". The lady said she'd be very happy to give this wee man a home ! A wise decision for both of us.

 I settled in well, very comfortable in the guest room, with a litter tray in the corner, newspapers over the good carpet, in case I made a mistake and didn't know what a litter tray was for. Mum had us well brought up, so we knew what litter trays were for, although this was a bit different from a shovel or two of garden soil in the corner ! I reckoned it was for the same purpose and no complaints were made !

 Herself and I were learning to adjust to each other and taking note of each other's habits. I learned quickly that she didn't like me helping her in the kitchen. She got quite cross when I was only trying to check that she hadn't bought any unnecessary shopping and that the butter was the right brand, when she was unpacking the groceries from the supermarket ------ or when I tried to help by licking dishes before she put them into the dishwasher. After that, I was banned from the kitchen. I didn't like her pulling my tail even though she wasn't hurting me, it's so undignified ! I wouldn't scratch or spit at her but I let her know that I don't like that childish kind of behavior. So I just flicked my tail in the air and walked away, groomed myself, licked my tail to perfection and hoped she got the message. All in all, we have come to a mutual understanding of our likes and dislikes.

She had kept me inside the house for quite a few months after I arrived, I didn't mind that a bit as it was Winter ----- cold, wet and windy outside ! Then, suddenly Spring and the longer evenings came, what was going to happen now, I wondered. Just before sundown we would take a walk around the garden, admire the flowers and I followed her closely at first, I wanted to be sure that she wouldn't go inside and close the door, forgetting all about me ! That became our evening routine, our special time out together and I learned a lot from her, such as don't even think about chasing the wee birds and don't pee in her rose beds !

Later on, when the warmer weather came, she decided that I should have my own apartment in the garage. It was a very interesting place, full of old bits of unwanted stuff that might come in handy someday. I spent quite a few nights in there (the car lived outside at the back door and never complained) but I was lonely, I missed the television and watching her at the computer. I used to take a nap on a chair beside the computer, and when I thought she was working too long at it and ignoring me, I used to jump on the keyboard and boy, that sure got her attention ! Usually she would laugh and say "OK, Charlie OK ! You're jealous, just let me finish this and then we'll have a break !"

By this time, she trusted me to go walkabout, usually to the beach at the bottom of the garden, although I soon found out that it was a good idea to come back home now and then to let her see me. I didn't have to go in, just jump up on the kitchen windowsill. On the long sunny summer evenings she didn't mind if I stayed out late, although on a few occasions she locked up, went to bed and didn't leave any supper for me ! After that, I'd appear home at a reasonable hour and that kept us both happy !

Nearly every day, the Missus' married daughter who lives not too far away, pops in to check that we are alright or need anything, have a chat and a quick cup of coffee with her Mum. Now that's really the highlight of my day too ! The daughter has TWO big golden retriever dogs, called Lewis and Ruby, actually they are auntie and nephew to each other and like children to her, but they are much more intelligent and obedient than any children I've ever seen ! We have become good mates and I do really enjoy their company, in spite of a natural suspicion that we cats have of dogs. The only problem is that they treat this house like their own, so I have to draw the line when they take this place for granted and let them know that I am the rightful owner here, well, partner.

Ruby sometimes likes to lie on a carpet mat that I like

to lie on. (I admit I don't lie on it often but visitors should be aware of owner's rights and property) So when she does, I just give her a good biff with my left paw and she soon vacates it. Lewis has a magnificent cream bushy tail and I can't help burying my face in it when he is quietly having a kip ------ Ooh, the smell of it is delightful ! Lewis doesn't seem to understand the pleasure it gives me. The minute he senses I'm enjoying his tail, he immediately jumps up and practically tramples me flat under his big feet and runs off to his Mummy ! Funny how a wee cat like me can scare the living daylights out of two huge (but well mannered) dogs like them. I do look forward to their daily visits. I can hear their car approach long before my Missus does, so I am on standby at the window watching and waiting for them.

    A couple of times in Autumn, when the evenings were shorter and a lot of my time seemed to be spent chasing leaves blowing in the wind, I thought I heard a meowing sound. Funny, I thought, because in all the time I've been out and about here, I have never seen or smelt another cat on my territory. Anyway, a few days later I spied what I thought was a mirror image of myself ----- Boy, did that spook me ! Couple of days later, I got another glimpse of this cat and later that afternoon, after a bit of viewing each other from a distance, we met casually on the beach.

    I discovered her name is Minnie, she's good-looking and she lives close by. Minnie is just as close to her family as I am to m'wee woman ! She is very happy with them in their seaside home. Now and again we meet up on the beach and have a good old chat and a dander, which suits us both. No point in us getting hitched, we discovered that we are both neutered and sure we don't want any more cats about here anyway ! It's nice to go home to your own place at night, supper waiting, no responsibilities other than making sure there's no mice around ! Life's pretty good. Cheers !

Big Boy Now

Charlie dear, please be careful on the road tonight, some of those cars drive far too fast and have absolutely no concern for pedestrians. Now, I don't mind you going out to meet up with your friends, I know it's only normal for a good-looking young fellow like you, but do stop, look and listen before you cross that busy road.

If you are in Warrenpoint and coming home late, have you thought about walking on the beach instead of on the road ? (When the tide is out, of course !) Sure, I know that you're not a good swimmer and you don't even like getting wet in the rain never mind salt water !!

I hear there are lots of good-looking girls around the Square in the Point ------- Ummm well, I'd rather you looked around the nice residential areas. Take a dander up the Well Road, into Clonallon and on down into Drumsesk. You could walk home that way and you never know who you might meet and have a chat with. You might meet some nice wee country girl, and I'm sure she'd be happy to meet a handsome well-mannered fellow like you. You could bring her home here anytime, for a meal. I'd like to meet her, and perhaps we could arrange somewhere for you both to live !! Sorry, sorry, sorry ! I'm jumping ahead too quickly, as usual. I keep forgetting that you're my beautiful wee baby black and white KITTEN !!! I do love you and like any mummy, I only want the best for you.

Further Reading

Eddie Joe

Eddie Joe the yardman was a bachelor of few words. He whistled to himself all the time as he went about the daily routine of seeing to the cattle, dunging out the byre, sweeping the yard and a hundred and one other things that fell on his shoulders. He had worked for the Campbells all his life and now in his later years this was the second generation of the family he served.

Eddie Joe was constantly shadowed by six-year-old Margaret, the youngest child, the wee late one and the apple of her Daddy's eye. She didn't mind when her questions weren't answered immediately, so she just asked Eddie Joe another one and waited patiently while he whistled away until he had finished what he was doing and leaned on the handle of his shovel to take a rest. Margaret told Eddie Joe all her worries knowing he would never tell anyone her secrets.

"Aye, that's right, Wee Meg", or "Don't you worry your wee head about it" or "There'll not be a word about it the day you're getting married", the same remarks repeated more or less summed up a year's conversation on his part.

Eddie Joe may have been a man of few words but he had a master's degree ------ in unspoken bad language ! Only to be used at full volume of course, in extreme provocation on anybody or anything that caused hurt or fear to an animal or caused Wee Margaret's tears to flow.

As I've told you this was a typical small Ulster farm where the father did the bulk of the work himself with the help of the "yardman". The children had their chores to do before and after school, that's just the way things were in those days before health and safety ruled the farm. Mammy saw to the children, the food, the homework, the shopping, the house, the hens, chickens, the garden and everything else that goes with a family of four boys ----- and a wee late girl born seven years after the last boy !

Rita was the daily help, a sturdy sixteen-year-old who did the endless washing, made the beds, mopped the floors, saw that the big range in the kitchen was kept well fueled, peeled the spuds for dinner and had an answer for everything !

Max, the farm collie lived outside in his kennel and well dare he, or either of the two black farm cats put their foot over the backdoor into the kitchen.

Friday afternoon usually saw their elderly spinster neighbour arrive up at the farm with her basket to buy fresh eggs, buttermilk and some nice fresh vegetables from Mrs. Campbell. Miss Agnew was a retired school teacher who took a keen interest in Wee Margaret's school work. After the business was done, Miss Agnew was always entertained in the front room to tea and biscuits (on the tray with the best china and the white linen embroidered tray cloth !) while she and Mrs. Campbell had their chat and caught up on local news. The only fly in the ointment was that Miss Agnew was always accompanied by Suzy, her Yorkshire terrier who wore a red tartan coat. Suzy had impeccable manners, was used to every degree of comfort and the finer things in life. When Miss Agnew was comfortably seated in the big chair by the fire, Suzy reclined on the sofa having graciously received her tidbit, Mrs. Campbell then poured the tea. This was a weekly procedure, all over in less than an hour with Miss Agnew and Suzy safely on their way home with their goodies.

Most days when Margaret came home from school full of chat and a bit tired, her mother tucked her up on the new sofa with a rug for a little rest. Some Friday afternoons were different, Miss Agnew could still be there when Margaret came in from school and that silly dog of hers was up on the good sofa ---- in the front room ---- IMAGINE !!

It was bad enough having to tell Miss Agnew all about what happened at school that day, what she had learned, how many pupils were off sick, without that silly dog lying up on the sofa watching her with a stupid grin on its face.

Time and time again, Eddie Joe was privy to the disgust and anger Wee Margaret felt about this dog. Miss Agnew was a teacher, and teachers ask questions all the time, Wee Margaret understood that alright but the dog allowed up on the new sofa and her mother just sat there smiling ? Oh, it was too much to bear !

When the summer holidays were over and the new

term started, sure enough on the first Friday Miss Agnew and Suzy arrived as usual. They were just about to leave when Wee Margaret came in from school, dropped her schoolbag in the hall and took one look into the front room. She drew herself up to her full height, marched into the room with arms akimbo, her wee face like thunder and with all the venom she could muster told Miss Agnew face to face, "Take yer swiggin' auld dog away home to shell or that !"

    Stunned silence.

Mrs. Morgan's Biscuits

Mrs. Morgan was one of those tiny elderly widow women, who had not had an easy life but was, as they say around here, "the heart of corn". She always pushed one of those old-fashioned tartan shopping trollies, which could be full or empty and used it as her walking aid. Walking sticks are only for dottery auld people and she hadn't reached that yet. "Thank God !" she would say.

    The girls in the shoe shop always looked forward to her chat when she came in, even if she was not buying anything. They knew she was getting a bit frail and her pension didn't go very far. She would call in often on Thursdays for a wee rest, before getting her groceries in the supermarket down the street. "The big shops don't have chairs for auld wimmen like me with sore feet", she'd say with a big laugh. "Sure they only want your money !"

    The shoe shop girls were always glad to see her for a bit of craic. She would reminisce about times past, when she bought all her shoes and those of her children in this shop and how much she paid for them. She could always remember all their boyfriend's names, where they liked to dance, the names of film stars, how the local football team was doing in the league or any bit of news around the town. She loved to go to watch any big society weddings in the Cathedral or any of the Protestant churches, as long as there was a bit of style and grandeur ! Next time when she called at the shop she would regale the girls about the latest wedding. The bride's dress in great detail, the bridesmaid's dresses, what mother of the bride wore, what the groom's mother wore, the suitability or unsuitability of the guest's apparel and the groom's good looks or otherwise ------ nothing escaped her notice !

Mrs. Morgan was a proud lady and while she liked to appear generous, the girls knew things were not easy, health wise or financially for her, anymore. Quite often if she was passing she would pop in, say hello, take a packet of biscuits or wee buns from her trolley with the instructions "That's for your elevenses, wee cup of tea, girls", leave them on the counter and disappear quickly.

When a pair of small cosy slippers was left too long in the shop window (and faded by the sun) the girls would ask, knowing they'd fit Mrs. Morgan perfectly, if she would have a use for them. "Sure we couldn't sell them in that state, the customers would complain, would you take them off our hands before the boss sees them ?" Mrs. Morgan would try them on and declare them the most comfortable millionaire's slippers she ever had seen or had on her feet !

In Winter, maybe a small pair of wide fitting waterproof shoes would appear, colour damaged and again Mrs. Morgan would benefit. Occasionally, she would buy shoe polish or cream or something for one of the many newborn babies in her extended family. That was fine, she was a good and trusted customer, just down on her luck a little.

The girls in the bakery shop across the street had a different slant on Mrs. Morgan. She always had a complaint about their goods, or in fact, everything ! They thought she was a difficult wee woman and tried not to have much chat with her. "Yer auld bread's always stale", she'd announce the minute she entered their shop, in front of other customers, knowing that would be repeated yet again in the bakery behind the shop.

"Well, why do you always buy it ?" the young apprentice would ask with a smile. Mrs. Morgan would just glower at her and turn away, pretending she didn't hear.

One morning, one of the office girls from the shoe shop had been to the bank on business and called at the bakery shop on her way back for some bread. Mrs. Morgan was already in there, seemingly in no hurry, walking around inspecting the cake and biscuit displays. The bakery shop assistant whispered to the office girl that she would attend to her in a minute but first she had to watch this old lady, as she was a prolific shoplifter, always stealing biscuits ! Take your eyes off of her and she'd have half the stock of cakes and biscuits in that tartan trolley and be off before you could blink !! Somehow, Mrs. Morgan's elevenses never tasted as good after that.

Them and Us

The battered old estate car bumped its way up the loanin, past the front of the once well-kept farmhouse with its overgrown front garden and jerked to a stop in the cobbled yard at the back.

All afternoon the ancient dog lay outside the kitchen half door in the late autumn sunshine. Between dreaming the dreams of much younger collie dogs, Barney heard the engine coming and was immediately on high alert. He took one look at the offending car, didn't bother to get up, bared his teeth and gave a few desultory barks just to let them see he was still a force to be dealt with, thus warning his beloved master who was dozing inside of impending doom.

The large lady disentangled herself from her seatbelt, reached for a package from the back seat while berating the man who was driving the car. "Thought we'd never get here James, you take too many chances, who taught you to drive anyway ? You have to concentrate more, and don't be looking over the hedges at cattle in the fields ! One of these days you'll have us both ------". She banged the door shut, strode up to the half door while poor James held back trying to look inconspicuous, letting his wife make their entrance.

"Helloooo ------ Uncle Arthur ------ Uncle Arthur ------ Yoo-hooo, guess who's come to see you ? Guess what I've brought for you, some of my very own homemade wheaten

bread !! Not too much for I know you don't eat a lot now ----
Ahh, there you are !!"

Old Arthur awoke with a jolt and realised the visitors were already in the kitchen standing beside him. That voice could only belong to his late sister's spoilt child but sure she was no child now, only a difficult, bossy old woman with a cowardly wee husband and a flock of vultures for children.

"God save us ! What have I done to deserve thon ones the day ?" he thought, "Bread she says, sure the last stuff even the crows wouldn't ate. I'd to brush it up in case it brought rats around the place ! They're after somethin' alright, for it's not for the love of me they're here. Even old Barney has no time for them."

"Come on in, sure it's nice to see you, there's many a day we don't see anybody at all. You'll excuse me if I don't get up, I've had a dose of this auld flu and it's hard to shake off. The years are there and this auld age isn't all it's cracked up to be when you're on your own !"

"Now now, Uncle, you're not looking too bad. I think you just need a bit of company, good food, regular meals and a bit of exercise and this place needs a good tidy up -----".

"Oh my God !" thought Arty, "Now I know what it is, me in a home and thon ones takin' over the place. Child dear, you've another thing comin' to you, for I'm goin' no place till they carry me out of here, boots first."

Madge glanced at the unshaven old man in his chair,

the untidy kitchen, piles of old yellowed newspapers, the scattered collection of post, some unopened and the stack dirty dishes all pushed to one end of the long table. She chose the least grubby chair, pushed it a little nearer Arty and sat down.

James hovered in the doorway, not quite sure if he should do the same or take a walk round the garden. "Poor Arthur" he thought, for he knew Madge was going to try yet again to persuade her uncle to make his mind up and go into sheltered housing. "The poor auld fella wouldn't last a week in there, with their rules and regulations and all those elderly widows on the lookout !"

Madge had plans for the old house and land. Their two sons had been a disappointment to them. Good-looking lads, who gave them no trouble but with no ambition to work or travel. As long as there was a roof over their heads, clean beds, food on the table and no rent to pay they were happy ! Everyone else had sons, (not half as handsome as theirs) who travelled the world, acquired endless degrees and qualifications, girlfriends and wives. Not that she would admit it to anyone but it hurt, now that they were coming up to thirty and still living at home. She would love to see them well set up, nice comfortable houses and cars, delightful wives and ------ some lovely talented grandchildren (oh yes please, but not too many !!)

"If we could move this old boy somewhere where he would be well looked after the boys could move in here, help tidy the place, new ideas and all that. I can just see it, new kitchen, a proper bathroom, the house all spruced up and painted, there's five bedrooms maybe with ensuites, they could do bed and breakfast ---- they could get a grant for that ---- a new Range Rover in the yard and even a sports car at the front door !! They could rent out the land, that would be more income !! Oh yes, that's the answer, James can't object to that ! 'Let them make their own way, in their own time', he says, but they need a good shove, I say."

"I'll make us a cup of tea, Uncle, you'd be ready for one I'm sure, no don't get up" Madge started to fill the old black kettle, find three reasonably clean cups, find the caddy and check if the milk wasn't off, "At least my bread is fresh" she thought !

By the time the tea was finished, light was fading and darkness drawing in. They settled by the fireside and made small talk, mostly about neighbours who had sold up or those who had died, the price of land and the mess the government was making for the farmers. Madge thought they were getting nowhere about the business they had come for and it was time to make another attempt before he fell asleep or asked them to leave.

The fire flickered, crackled and slipped into a lower gear. White ash gained a little ground and the kitchen shadows deepened. Barney stretched his full length on the old, tatted hearth rug and opened one eye. "Aww jaypers, she's still at it" he thought, as the woman's voice wheedled and droned on and on.

"We all think it's the right thing to do Arthur, sure you'll not know yourself ------- no sticks and turf to carry in and your dinner set up to you. No worrying about leaks in the roof or the spuds never out of the ground and you able to click your fingers and say 'Where's my tay ?' Now think about it seriously Arthur, sure we all want the best for you."

Barney's one eye swept over the three faces. He saw the greedy glint behind the woman's glasses and her husband's look of approval. He saw the tight grip of old hands on the arms of his chair and the pallor on the old face. "The auld boy's tired" he thought, "That's it, I've had enough. I'll have to shift these ones ------ time they were away home anyway." He sighed, scratched and sent up a silent but noxious odour and waited for the reactions !!

"Ooh ------- Dear dear, is it that the time already ?" said Madge, scrabbling in her sleeve for her hanky. James coughed and spluttered, he quickly jumped up and reached for their coats hanging beside the door, at the same time opening it to let in a blast of cold fresh air. Madge struggled with her coat and covered her nose with her hanky. "Now Arthur ----- think about what I said, sure I'll see to everything for you. No Uncle Arthur, no, please don't get up, we'll see ourselves out. Good night, God bless and I'll come and see you again soon."

"You'll not bloody well see to me, Missus !" thought Barney, "I'll see to him and I'll see to me. We don't need the likes of you pushin' in here." The fire hissed goodnight at the pair of them as old Arty damped it down with a shovel of damp slack from the bucket in the corner beside the firewood. He shook his finger at Barney, "I know what you were up to, old boy ! Right, out you go and don't be long about it, I'm ready for me bed !"

Barney took a look around outside, cocked his leg at the iron gate, checked that the five hens were on the roost, the cats settled in the empty barn, no sign of the fox and all was well. He slipped back into the house and lay on his mat behind the door. "Phew !" thought Barney, "That's enough for one day."

Old Arty slept fitfully throughout the long night. "It's only three in the morning" he thought. "Many's a time I was only comin' in at this time, grumblin' about havin' to get up at five to do the milkin' ---- God, I wish I could do it all again ! ----- Indeed, no I do not, sure I wouldn't be fit for it, it was hard work. Maybe they're right, I should be in a home and sign the place over to them, at least it would be goin' to kith and kin. They mean well, maybe I'll go and see the solicitor in the morning."

At four o'clock he was thinking that maybe it wasn't such a good idea after all and in a week or two, when he'd get his strength back he would buy a few cattle in the Spring. Wouldn't that give him a bit of interest in his affairs ?

As the luminous hands of his wee clock crept up to five o'clock, Arty's brain was working overtime. "Maybe if I was over this wee turn and looked after myself a bit better, I could spend a bit of money and get this place tidied up ------ by the hokey, I might buy myself a new suit !! Sure what would hinder me goin' into the town on a Saturday evenin' and havin' a bite to eat in the hotel ? There's the tourin' busses from Scotland comin' in on a Saturday, maybe there'd be a wee Scotch widow woman or some other sensible woman who'd be keen to meet a fella like me ! Sure, I was a quare dago in my day, couldn't I have married many's the time only for the Mammy, and her poorly ? Boys I say, I could go yet, so I could ! I tell you, that would give them something to talk about. Thon niece of mine would just love to get her hands on this house and bit of land to pass on to that crowd of yahoos of hers. Well, she just might have another thing comin'. Anyway, what would I do about Barney ? Who'd want a crabbit auld mongrel like that ? No, he'd better stay on here with me, we'll manage OK."

    Arty gave a sigh of relief, drifted off to sleep and in his dreams sauntered out of the farm gate and headed for the town in his new suit and fancy brown brogues, whistling "The Wild Rover", leaving Barney to look after the place as usual.

The Flowers in May

Mary loved flower arranging. She'd even been to a few classes over the years but she knew she'd never make a florist. She loved working with spring flowers best of all. She loved the fragile white snowdrops that burst through after the long Winter, the smell of the first daffodils, the heady smell and colour of the pink and blue hyacinths. Early spring sunshine, birds nesting and the riotous colours of the stately tulips made her sing with joy. Mary was happy.

The kitchen was a mess with flowers piled in heaps on the table, bits of bare branches and greenery littered the floor and Frank Sinatra was singing his heart out on her old record player.

She had just finished a big haphazard arrangement of daffodils, narcissus and anything else she could find in bloom when her friend Vera popped in to see if she would like to go shopping in the afternoon. Vera was a very kind person really, good neighbour, nothing was too much trouble for her if she could help but Vera was a perfectionist in everything she did ------ or thought she was !

"Good grief, Mary ! What kind of a haystack is that you're making ? Why did you not start with some oasis at the bottom and then it wouldn't be all lopsided ? Why are you using all those bits of sticks and where on earth did you find that old cracked jug ? Here, let me tidy this up a bit."

Mary's face crumpled, "I knew it, I knew it" she thought, "I'm just no good at anything !" and all the pleasure she had felt earlier disappeared.

Vera proceeded to dismantle Mary's work. Every flower was extracted, every branch laid on the table according to size. She demanded an oasis, knowing it was doubtful if Mary had any. "How could anyone attempt to arrange flowers without it ?" She demanded a nice container, knowing Mary had some lovely old antique vases "Nothing cracked or dirty, thank you ! How could Mary work without proper secateurs ? These old scissors are blunt, absolutely no use for this job. Always start with the right equipment and then everything will fall into place", she said.

Mary stood behind her like a good pupil, watching sadly as Vera, with a few deft thrusts, positioned about half the branches and a quarter of the lovely flowers into the new container, making the arrangement look as if it was still growing in the garden. "There you are, Mary, that's what I always say ------ less is more !"

"Thank you, Vera. I'll try to remember all that. I'm really sorry I can't go shopping with you this afternoon, I'm rather busy. Perhaps another day when it suits, thank you for asking me." Then Mary smiled to herself ----- "When this 'paragon' goes I'll wreck the whole bloody lot, gather more flowers and sing along with Frank's 'I Did It My Way'" !!

Mr. McBride's Big Moment

Mr. McBride edged his wee red car into the supermarket car park. He found a handy space, backed in, pulled on the handbrake and switched her off. He reached for his paper, pushed his seat back, adjusted his spectacles and made himself comfortable. The familiar "Won't be long, dear" didn't come. Panic hit John James McBride like a ten-ton truck. "Aww jaypers, it's me", he thought. "Sod this for a carry on !" He took several long deep breaths and fished the shopping list from his pocket:

Tea bags   1/2 lb.   Butter   Bacon (back)

Carrots   Potatoes (pink)   Brown bread milk (semi)

    All written out in Mrs. McBride's neat hand. "Seven items", he thought, "Shouldn't take long. Nothing to it ----- easy as wee buns. Nothing to it. Mmmm—wee buns ! Wee buns would be nice specially the ones they make here, but sure Margaret always makes wee buns on a Saturday. 'Bought buns are far too dear' she says, 'Don't forget we're pensioners now !'"

    "Ahh jeepers, there'll be no buns this week --- not with the leg in plaster ! Why didn't she look where she was going ? Amn't I always telling her ? Look where you're going, woman, would you take it easy, you're not as young as you used to be !"

"Get on or that with you – you auld git !" always the same answer. "Ahh Margaret, Margaret. Six weeks, that young skelp of a doctor told us. 'You'll be a great help to your wife now that you have retired.' Nothing to do but dance attendance on her all day ! 'She'll be good as new when she gets her plaster off in six weeks.' SIX WEEKS ? Six bloody weeks ! Sure what would he know about it anyway ? He looks as if he should be out playing football !"

Mr. McBride checked his list again, patted his wallet, got out and locked the car, opened it up again and retrieved the list from the passenger seat. "Well, this is it, Johnny boy ! A whole new set up for you", he thought. "Duty calls and I'm as good a man as the next !" Mr. McBride looked around the car park. Several couples of a certain age were pushing loaded trolleys and chatting with each other. "'Tame husbands', Margaret calls them. She doesn't mind me sitting in the car waiting for her. 'Men are only a hindrance in supermarkets', she says, 'They question the price of everything and ask stupid questions. She sees it all the time. 'They should be left outside or at home', she says."

A husband and wife trundled their load up to the car beside him. "Good Morning" said Mr. McBride, just being friendly, but his voice came out high pitched and squeaky. The other man opened the boot of his car and slung in a few bags of groceries while the wife settled herself into her seat and opened a bag of crisps. "Get in there quick, man, before all the English caulies go", he gave Mr. McBride a conspiratorial nod.

"Oh God ! What kind of a set-up is this ?" panicked John James. "Sure haven't we a ceasefire ? ---- Could it be a farewell party for the Paras ? ---- Am I safe ? Man dear, would you wise up, look pleasant and walk on." He took several deep breaths. All the same, he gave a quick skelly round the car park. All seemed to be well, not a caulie in sight ------ whoever they were !

Near the entrance stood two long rows of trollies, all neatly chained together. Mr. McBride remembered that Margaret always had a pound coin ready. He hoked in his pocket, found one and marched confidently up to the trollies. He looked for a slot. No slot. Mr. McBride adjusted his spectacles and examined the trolley. He adjusted his spectacles again and began a more thorough investigation.

"How the Hell ?" he thought to himself. Suddenly a child appeared at the other row, with a deft click-click unhooked a trolley from its mates and made off at a rate of knots towards mother standing nearby. "Well, this bloody thing won't beat me", thought John James.

"Place coin ------" he read, but the instructions had rubbed off a bit. Mr. McBride scratched his bald patch as he always did in an emergency. "Am I stupid or what ? Wouldn't you think they would fix it ? I'm getting too old for all this technology."

Just then a lady appeared returning her empty trolley to the dock. "Here, have mine" she said, smiling. Mr. McBride mumbled his thanks and turned away with it. "Hey

Mister, what about my pound ?" her tone had changed. "Some people would take the eye out of your head !" Mr. McBride handed over his pound sheepishly. "Sorry about that, Missus, my mistake, the wife you know ----". She gave him a withering look, "You couldn't watch auld fellas" was her parting shot at him.

      Mr. McBride gave a sigh. "That's the first hurdle over now", he thought. "Chin up, shoulders back and look happy. Here we go, here we go, here we go-oooh." Off the pair of them went, heading for the automatic doors, with his trolley leading the way ---- sideways !!

D'Ye Mind the Day ?

When you fell out of the big tree ? We were looking for bird's nests, you split your head and cut your knee, then you ran home and told Mummy that I pushed you. You KNEW that we were not allowed to climb that big tree !

When we chased Mrs. What's-her-name's chickens down to the river. You said chickens had built in radar like cats, they'd find their own way home after they had their swim. Their radar didn't work that day.

When Uncle Fred got his new Ford Popular car. You said if we put some fresh water into the petrol tank it would go twice as fast for him. It didn't.

When the neighbours got their new swimming pool, you said that it would look better if it had a few stones in the bottom of it, then it would look more like the seaside. They didn't think so.

When we helped the lady next door by pulling all her Victoria plums for her, she had told Mum she was going to make jam with them soon. The plums just needed another two or three weeks to ripen.

When our wee friend Margaret got a sore tummy when she came to play after school, so we made her a hot drink with California syrup of figs mixed with some of Daddy's whiskey. Her Mummy said she'll be OK tomorrow when she gets out of hospital.

When you discovered that we couldn't make sandcastles from the four large packets of washing powder emptied onto the kitchen floor and mixed with cups of water. It took longer than you thought to clear it all up before we were allowed to have dinner.

When we dressed Tilly the cat up for Christmas with Mum's good pearls ? she ran away up the garden and came home without them. Mum found them when she was planting lettuce in the Springtime.

No, I won't forget it either !

Some Old Cures from Mourne !

A few of those in the community were people who used their powers and did not accept payments. They did not quite understand why they had the "gift" but treated it with respect and a blessing to be shared. Individuals said to have the "cure" were: the seventh son of a seventh son; husbands and wives with the same surname before marriage.

Sore throat - Have a cabbage leaf tied around the throat overnight.

Bad cough - Take a half cup of docken seeds, washed, put in a saucepan and cover with cold water, bring to the boil and simmer for ten minutes, leave until cold. Take a tablespoon when cough is troublesome.

Sprains - Goose fat rubbed on the sprain.

Warts - Cut a small turnip in two, rub one half on the warts, sprinkle with sugar and put in a glass jam-jar, leave in a dark place and don't ever look at it again until the warts have disappeared.

Bleeding - Spread a clean cobweb on the wound.

Stings - Remove sting barb if possible. Bathe with a strong solution of bicarbonate of soda or use a bluebag (used to whiten cloth) dipped in water.

To purify the blood - Used once a year. Take a little bit of soot from the chimney, mix with some milk and honey. One teaspoon taken for two mornings by all the children in the family.

Sore stomach - Mustard plaster. Take 1 tablespoon mustard mixed with the white of one egg. Spread on to a piece of brown paper and cover with a clean white cloth. Apply on stomach for about an hour, avoid keeping it on longer.

When You Think About It !

Age is not important, unless you are a cheese.

Bucket seats: Not everyone has the same size bucket.

Buffet: A French word that means "Get up and get it yourself".

Hindsight: Sitting on your glasses (by mistake of course !)

Laughing stock: Cattle with a sense of humour.

If the world is getting smaller why does the postal rate keep going up ?

Patience is the ability to let your light shine after your fuse has blown.

Where do they get the seeds to grow seedless oranges ?

Isn't it incredible that news from all over the world fits exactly into the newspaper !

Isn't it a bit unnerving that doctors call what they do "practice" ?

Before credit cards we always knew exactly how much we were broke.

Duty makes us do things well but love makes us do them beautifully.

The only thing wrong with doing nothing is that you never know when you have finished.

If you see someone without a smile give them one of yours !

(Author unknown)

Bible Cake Recipe

Ingredients:

8 oz Judges	Ch. 5 v. 25	Butter
8 oz 1 Samuel	Ch. 30 v. 12	Raisins
1 tbsp 1 Samuel	Ch. 14 v. 25	Honey
16 oz 1 Kings	Ch. 4 v. 22	Plain flour
3 tsp Amos	Ch. 4 v. 5	Baking powder
8 oz Jeremiah	Ch. 6 v. 20	Sugar
3 oz Jeremiah	Ch. 17 v. 11	Eggs
2 oz Nahum	Ch. 3 v. 12	Figs
2 oz Numbers	Ch. 17 v. 8	Blanched almonds
1 tsp Exodus	Ch. 35 v. 28	Spice
Judges	Ch. 4 v. 19	Milk

Method:

Preheat oven to 325 F. Gas 3, 160 C. Grease and line 9" round tin.

Cream Judges 5 v. 25 and Jeremiah 6 v. 20. Beat 1 Samuel 14 v. 25 with Jeremiah 17 v. 11. Add to Judges and Jeremiah with a little 1 Kings 4 v. 22. Mix remainder of 1 Kings with

Amos 4 v. 5 (leaven), 1 Samuel 30 v. 12, Nahum 3 v. 12 (chopped), Numbers 17 v. 8 (chopped) and Exodus 35 v. 28.

Fold the 1 Kings mixture into the Judges and Jeremiah with enough Judges 4 v. 19 to make a dropping consistency. Put cake mix in tin, scooping out a hollow in the centre. Bake for about 1 hour 30 minutes or until cooked.

Cool on a wire tray, decorate with royal icing when cold and top with some Numbers Ch. 17 v. 8 (chopped and roasted).

(From "Cathedral Cuisine – A Cookbook from the Catholic Diocese of Baton Rouge")

Printed in Great Britain
by Amazon